Francesco Clemente: Three Worlds

This exhibition and catalogue are supported
by generous grants from The Pew Charitable Trusts,
the National Endowment for the Arts,
and The Bohen Foundation, with additional
support from Alitalia Italian Airlines
and the Italian Ministry of Foreign Affairs.

Francesco Clemente
Three Worlds

Ann Percy and Raymond Foye
*with essays by Stella Kramrisch
and Ettore Sottsass*

Organized by Ann Percy

Philadelphia Museum of Art
Rizzoli, New York

Itinerary of the Exhibition

Philadelphia Museum of Art
October 20—December 23, 1990

Wadsworth Atheneum, Hartford
January 27—March 17, 1991

San Francisco Museum of Modern Art
April 11—June 2, 1991

First trade edition published in the United States of
America in 1990 by
Rizzoli International Publications, Inc.
300 Park Avenue South, New York, New York 10010

Printed and bound in Italy

Library of Congress Cataloging-in-Publication Data
Percy, Ann.
Francesco Clemente : three worlds / Ann Percy and
Raymond Foye ; with essays by Stella Kramrisch and
Ettore Sottsass ; exhibition organized by Ann Percy.
p.   cm.
Catalogue of an exhibition held at the Philadelphia
Museum of Art, Oct. 20–Dec. 23, 1990; Wadsworth
Atheneum, Hartford, Jan. 27–March 17, 1991; San
Francisco Museum of Modern Art, April 11–June 2,
1991.
Includes index.
ISBN 0-87633-084-7 (Philadelphia Museum).
ISBN 0-8478-1297-9 (Rizzoli)
1. Clemente, Francesco, 1952–   —Exhibitions.
I. Foye, Raymond, 1957–   . II. Kramrisch, Stella,
1896–   . III. Sottsass, Ettore, 1917–   .
IV. Philadelphia Museum of Art.   V. Title.
NC257.C575A4   1990
709'.2—dc20   90-45673
                                              CIP

Contents

Lenders to the Exhibition

Thomas Ammann, Zurich

Art & Project, Slootdorp, The Netherlands

Francesco and Alba Clemente, New York

Crown Point Press, San Francisco and New York

Anthony d'Offay Gallery, London

Gerald S. Elliott, Chicago

Wolfgang Max Faust, Berlin

Raymond Foye, New York

Henry Geldzahler, New York

Judy and Harvey Gushner, Bryn Mawr, Pennsylvania

IFIDA Health Care Group, Bryn Mawr, Pennsylvania

Ronald Krueck, Chicago

Helen N. Lewis and Marvin B. Meyer, Beverly Hills

Joshua Mack, Byram, Connecticut

Paul Maenz, Cologne

Collection Mis, Brussels

The Museum of Modern Art, New York

Öffentliche Kunstsammlung Basel, Kupferstichkabinett

PaineWebber Group Inc., New York

Francesco Pellizzi, New York

Marcello Pepori, Arosio, Italy

Petersburg, London and New York

Philadelphia Museum of Art

Jean Pigozzi, Lausanne

Barbara Radice, Milan

Collection Sanders, Amsterdam

Joan Sonnabend, Boston

Sperone Westwater, New York

Marion Stroud Swingle, Elverson, Pennsylvania

Virginia Museum of Fine Arts, Richmond

Alan Wanzenberg, New York

Private Collections

Private Collection, Courtesy Galerie Bruno Bischofberger, Zurich

Foreword

It should come as no surprise that an exhibition devoted to the work of Francesco Clemente over the past twenty years should prove a remarkably international enterprise. With loans from collections in many countries and contributions to this catalogue from an Italian designer and architect, an American publisher, and an Austrian-born curator and scholar of Indian art, this project presents an extraordinary range of works on paper by an artist who has consistently drawn his inspiration from the culture, both ancient and contemporary, of the places in which he has lived and worked: most notably Italy, Madras, and New York.

One of an ongoing sequence of monographic exhibitions organized by the Philadelphia Museum of Art devoted to the work of contemporary artists, this project owes much to the generosity and forbearance of many lenders, whose enthusiasm for Clemente's work is matched by their willingness to part with loans over an extended period of time. We are deeply grateful to The Pew Charitable Trusts, the National Endowment for the Arts, and The Bohen Foundation for their support of the exhibition and its catalogue, and to the Italian Ministry of Foreign Affairs for additional assistance, received through the good offices of the Italian Consulate in Philadelphia. The project has also received welcome support from Alitalia Italian Airlines. This handsome book, designed by Nathan Garland and produced with flair by George H. Marcus and his staff in the Publications Department of the Philadelphia Museum of Art, is concurrently published in the United States by Rizzoli International, and a profound debt of thanks is owed to Alfredo de Marzio, Chairman of Rizzoli Corporation, New York, who not only gave this project warm encouragement from the beginning of his involvement but has also been of assistance in many ways.

It is a pleasure to thank the several authors of essays in this catalogue, each of whom has contributed his or her own distinctive vision of Clemente's art, and we do so most warmly together with Ann Percy, Curator of Drawings at the Museum, herself an author as well as *primum mobile* of the exhibition as it has developed over the past six years.

Ann Percy's admiration for things Italian extends with scholarship and ease from the seventeenth-century Naples of Bernardo Cavallino to the art of the present day, as she has so capably demonstrated in the organization and selection of the exhibition. We join her in expressing thanks to our colleagues at the Wadsworth Atheneum in Hartford and the San Francisco Museum of Modern Art, whose participation in the exhibition tour ensures it a wide audience. Suzanne F. Wells, Special Exhibitions Coordinator, Martha S. Small, Associate Registrar, and Sherry Babbitt, Editor in the Publications Department, have devoted much skill and energy respectively to the arrangements for the exhibition and its tour and the preparation of the catalogue manuscript.

It is above all a delight to express our gratitude to Francesco Clemente for his patience, invaluable help, and unfailing courtesy over the past six years. It has been a profound pleasure for the Museum staff to work with him during the entire process of creating this exhibition.

Anne d'Harnoncourt
The George D. Widener Director

Innis Howe Shoemaker
*Senior Curator of Prints,
Drawings, and Photographs*

Acknowledgments

The Philadelphia Museum of Art first became interested in organizing a show of Francesco Clemente's works on paper in 1984, when we acquired one of his pastels and began to be aware of the range and power of his production in various mediums. During the several years before the project's realization, the Museum's Director, Anne d'Harnoncourt, has been enthusiastic in her support of it. In the course of researching and selecting the works for the exhibition, many colleagues have been particularly helpful. Rainer Crone, who has written extensively on Clemente, kindly made available the large photographic archive that he compiled documenting Clemente's work up to 1984, which was an invaluable resource. Angela Westwater and her staff at Sperone Westwater in New York provided access to the thorough bibliographical files on the artist accumulated by the gallery and have aided in the locating of many works, as has Marie-Louise Laband at the Anthony d'Offay Gallery in London. Michael Auping offered helpful advice at the beginning stages of the project, and Christina Houssian contributed expert and invaluable research assistance.

A great many people have helped in making works available, supplying photographs and information, and handling loan requests: I would particularly like to thank Vigna Antoniniana, Angelo Baldassarre, Douglas Baxter, Monique Beudert, Tanya Bonakdar, Frederick R. Brandt, Maria Brassel, James Burden, Michael Conforti, Anstiss Drake, Tracy Goodnow, Thomas D. Grischkowsky, Franziska Heuss, Pontus Hulten, Mary Jacoby, Dieter Koepplin, Linda Kratz, Sonia L. Lopez, Karen McCready, Eileen Maciewski, Joshua Mack, Jane MacNichols, Emilio Mazzoli, Massimo Minini, Adriaan van Ravesteijn, Mera and Donald Rubell, Kathy and Keith Sachs, Johanna Schultheiss, Lloyd Speed, Robin Vousden, Gerd de Vries, Wendy Weitman, and Richard B. Woodward. Our colleagues at the institutions participating in the show have been of much assistance as well, particularly Linda Ayres and Andrea Miller-Keller at the Wadsworth Atheneum, and Barbara Levine at the San Francisco Museum of Modern Art.

Several Museum colleagues have been called on often for advice over the years, in particular Mark Rosenthal, Ann Temkin, Ellen S. Jacobowitz, John Ittmann, and Innis Howe Shoemaker. The Museum's Rights and Reproductions and Photography Departments have coped with a mountain of photography, and I am most grateful to Conna Clark, Graydon Wood, Andrew Harkins, and Terry Flemming-Murphy for their efforts. Conservators Denise Thomas and Faith H. Zieske provided much helpful advice; Christine G. Baumann and Rhonda Davis compiled endless lists and their revisions; Anita Gilden, Gina B. Erdreich, and Lilah J. Mittelstaedt gave library assistance; David W. Wolfe helped work out the exhibition's installation design; and Phoebe Toland resolved problems of matting and framing. With care and zeal far beyond the call of duty, Sherry Babbitt has guided the catalogue through the editorial process.

I am above all grateful to my collaborator and coauthor Raymond Foye for the many invaluable services he has provided to the exhibition and catalogue and for the fine intelligence with which he has provided them, as well as to Stella Kramrisch for her vital connection with the exhibition and its artist from the beginning, which has served, as does Clemente's own work, to conjoin East and West, present and past, word and image.

Ann Percy
Curator of Drawings

Francesco: Libertine of Mysteries

Ettore Sottsass

Francesco told me that the spiders of Jamaica came to greet him all dressed up in a procession because he had done a painting of a spider who was the king of the island.

Francesco never says stupid things when he talks. I mean he never says boring things, he doesn't tell me what time his plane left for somewhere or other, he doesn't tell me how late his flight was or even whether it was raining or sunny.

Francesco at five o'clock one morning in August went onto the roof of the house on Filicudi and watched the silence of the night dying and the dawn rising behind the volcanoes of Sicily; he recited a mantra and then came down to protest because the evening before we had lost a long game of cards that had been won, of course, by that pair of horrible women, Alba and Barbara.

So Francesco has never talked to me about paper or about different sorts of paper; still less have we talked about Italy as a general place, and we have talked even less about the relation between painting on paper and the phantom of Italy and things like that. Perhaps once, in India, Francesco talked about the paper they make at Pondicherry. At that time Francesco was in India and painting on paper. On the floor of a big, empty room he had a whole mass of painted, beautiful paper. But Francesco has never talked to me about his drawings on paper. I don't know anything about Francesco's paintings on paper.

At this point, if the Philadelphia Museum asked me, I could better describe how Francesco covered his head with a wet towel at two in the afternoon in a boat in the middle of the Mediterranean Sea under a scorching sun, to look more handsome and fascinating or maybe to look like a poor sadhu, with a lump of sugar and a basil leaf in the palm of one hand. This I could describe.

Certainly I find it, I won't say difficult but perhaps impossible, to describe any decision by Francesco concerning his drawings or paintings on paper. However, for the Philadelphia Museum and — I hope — for a smile from Francesco, I can invent something. Why shouldn't I invent something? Don't we go ahead by dint of metaphors?

For example, I could say that in Italy the culture of paper is much the same as it is in India: there are craftsmen or small mills dotted about that make special kinds of paper, all-cotton handmade paper, as they say, heavy, dry, granular paper that absorbs just the right amount of water, paper that lets watercolor spread and makes it transparent, or opaque; soft paper that can be picked up and laid on the table as if it were a religious instrument.

This happens in Italy and it happens in India, as it happens perhaps in Japan or other places I don't know about. In any case this idea of making precious special paper is about the last esoteric suburb of paper "culture"; it's a kind of final abstraction of the conditions, the limits, the mythologies, and the orgasms that ordinary people, in different places, have produced on the subject of paper culture.

In Italy, as in many other places, machine-made paper, industrial paper, and paper for newspapers, magazines, books, and miscellaneous advertising is made, and all this paper, suitable for machines, rotary presses, slow and fast printing, is also exported to other countries.

But this industrial paper, all this compact, shiny, white, crackly, heavy, plastified paper, doesn't seem to be able in even the slightest bit to contaminate that general way, that stupid way, that daily way of using paper, of holding it, throwing it away, burning it, pasting it, cutting it, honoring it, and despising it, which concerns the popular culture of paper, the culture that circulates in the senseless hours of days and nights, the culture of paper to be found in alleys and in *trattorias,* in train stations, at the grocer's and the butcher's, at the dairy and in the pastry shop, at the post office and maybe also in the ministries; certainly in army barracks and in the official gazette, but also in porno photofiction.

In India too the popular culture of paper is at a standstill on the yellow cigarette packets, on the election notices that hang from the whorehouses of Bombay, on the prints with saints, the divine lovers, the gods, the snakes, the elephants, the monkeys, the cut-off heads, the lotus flowers, the white sunsets, the dawns.

In all these wide popular uses, paper, being expensive stuff, has to cost less and less, and so for popular uses the paper gets thinner and thinner and more transparent, grayer and yellower, more violet-colored, dirtier and coarser. They put less and less cotton (which costs money) in it and more and more rags instead, and mixed leaves, torn stockings, scraps of wood, old newspapers; anything that can be made into a pulp that later turns into paper.

Sometimes I get letters from India on such thin paper that you can hardly touch it. As soon as I open the envelope (very slowly in case it all falls to pieces), the letter inside blows away and I have to chase it through the air.

On the island of Filicudi, there were almost no scraps of paper flying about as there are in all other places. Paper was too expensive; it wasn't used, or if it was, it was so light that it blew straight away into the sea.

I mean only for a few, very few years now in Italy have those heaps of small and large brown boxes with expanded polystyrene in them been around, that are used to wrap up refrigerators, bicycles, bottles of wine or whiskey, hi-fis, terminals, loudspeakers, cameras, anything.

In Italy, until a short while ago, if you had to deliver a chair to somebody you made a wooden cage tied up with string, or if the journey was a short one it would be wrapped in a gray blanket. Packages were made with light, crumbly paper that was always too short, and Romanengo in Genoa, who used to sell the best chocolates in the world, made his packets with a blue, shiny paper, whereas butchers used yellow paper with dirty, very vulgar black spots on it, and sugar was put in gray-blue paper bags that were always falling apart, and fruit, lettuce, or tomatoes were sold in old newspaper. Almost all packets were made of newspaper; even your shoes mended by the cobbler, even books, even bread, was taken home wrapped in old newspaper; whereas for oranges there was a very thin paper printed with the growers' trademarks, which were always figures of heroes from a long popular dream: lions, tigers, Garibaldi, Aïda, Othello, the occasional special dragon, gigantic snakes, sometimes even printed in gold.

Then all the paper would be thrown away.

I don't know where it went. Perhaps it ended up against walls, and on very windy days it fluttered and blew through the streets, then got caught in the corners of wet alleyways or finished up against the wire netting round vegetable gardens, or even in the middle of sculptures in cemeteries, and all these millions of bits of paper ended up here and there scattered across the landscape; the butcher's blood-stained yellow paper, the whitish blue sugar paper, the newspaper soggy from squashed tomatoes, the newspaper green with basil leaves or black with squashed grapes or overripe plums.

Millions of shreds of paper blew here and there, all over the place, wet with rain, dried up by the sun, slowly losing their original colors, very slowly dissolving and leaving traces of their existence for a long time and then slowly disappearing, slowly vanishing into the grass, into the bushes, into the earth.

That thin, flying paper, those bits of paper that cost nothing and were worth nothing, those shreds of newspapers that had announced immense wars, or ordinary births, or triumphal victories, or unexpected inventions, ridiculous scandals or calamities of every description and equally frequent idiocies, or those other bits of paper that had wrapped sweet Sunday pastries, and the other bits that had wrapped old mended shoes, left here and there, for a long time, the faintest shadow of what had happened.

All those pieces of paper left a kind of dead silent warning on the subject of the general ambiguity of events, of the general doubleness of connections between events, even about the actual dusty material that the events are made of; a material always liable to vanish with breathing. Like the dust of pastels on paper? Like certain uncertain lines or signs only just visible, abandoned lines, with no spaces to join them together, lines ready to disappear at once?

I may be very wrong, but I can't help thinking that those Italian landscapes of processions with wobbly saints, with tall plumes of incense, along streets paved with rose petals and closed by skies of gentle paper flags, that those interiors decorated with Catholic paper festoons, those interiors of such modest wealth and such modest festivity, may also simply describe nothing but the perception of global existential frailty, that they are nothing but uncertain landscapes, paper stage designs in fact, acting as backcloths to imagined, fleeting dramatic apparitions rather than heavy stage sets, rather than stone backdrops to final dramas.

Maybe the Italians, I mean the Italians of the alleyways, the Italians of the shops, the Italians of the long streets, the Italians of the boats, the Italians of the soccer team, the Italians who stick up posters with half-naked women on them, the Italians who sit all day long, the Italians who work as waiters, I mean that part of the Italians who are *simpatici*, who keep life going, perhaps those Italians, cannot even begin to imagine the existence either of final dramas or even, still less, of stone stage designs, to act as backdrops to final dramas.

Those Italians, those endearing, friendly, wise Italians and ancient mariners of the seas of life, those ancient technologists of magic, need only a bit of paper. A piece of paper with faded colors, stretched like a sky over the street, is all they need to get to heaven straight-away, from four till six in the afternoon. Even just a bit of moldy paper — blue with a few chocolates in it — is enough to finish, for half an hour or so, in the heaven of bed; you only need a scrap of paper for a few words of love, only a scrap of paper to write down songs, only a double newspaper to cheat customers with the weighing machine, and then life is so frail, so tender that it only takes flying signs, a few signs drawn in the air, signs with the hands, signs with the fingers, signs with the eyes are enough, at times a sigh, a hoarse cry, is enough to touch existence.

Francesco, too, a perplexed Italian, an astute Italian, a libertine of mysteries, only needs a few small pieces of paper, I mean he only needs paper as a small piece of existence, to fly up to paradise, to climb up to the sky, even to end up in a bed, to enter the belly of women, to wallow in the general amusement park of existence, to chase and to sign, to tell us, heaven knows how, about the logic of thoughts that for some reason aren't logical, about the logic of visions that certainly aren't logical, the logic of memories, nostalgias, complexes, desires that all together, memories, nostalgias, complexes, desires, have absolutely no clear connections, are not laid down in recognizable layers, not even as we — calmly — stroll and think about life, and not even when at times perhaps we also feel content.

To mark these uncertain states, to give existence to combinations without logic, to throbbing apparitions, illuminations and darknesses, intersections, falls and endless orgasms, to mark out somewhere this strange perception that the sperm of life comes out of the veins, the hands, the eyes, the skull, the sex, very slowly, gently, spreading all around, perhaps there is only air, or perhaps there are only these flimsy bits of paper, this paper that costs nothing, this flying paper, this paper that settles on your hands like dust.

So far as I know, Francesco, with this Italian paper, when he was very small and then afterward, always came to this conclusion: to knowing that life, ancient life, our life, is a fragile, gentle, uncertain thing. Like cheap paper, it drifts here and there and every now and again works in a shady room and every now and again falls onto the ground and lets itself be absorbed by the earth.

Locale

Raymond Foye

The local is not a place but a place in a given man—what part of it he has been compelled or else brought by love to give witness to in his own mind. And that is THE form, that is, the whole thing, as whole as it can get.

I think we will be fools to be embarrassed by it. We know the other neatness possible, the way of the neat pattern, and the dodging which it must call for. Grace has no part in that. At some point reached by us, sooner or later, there is no longer much else but ourselves, in the place given us. To make that present, and actual for other men, is not an embarrassment, but love.
Robert Creeley*

In the early 1970s Francesco Clemente began a series of migrations between Italy, India, and New York that continues to this day. Indeed, the itinerant nature of his career is one of its chief characteristics. He has traced a path between three cities—Rome, Madras, New York—each a fulcrum for interrelated yet distinct activities shaped by the individual character, history, and geography of the locale. Subjects, materials, and working methods are, for Clemente, inextricably bound to a simple fact: geography. These specifics of place have always been a determining factor for Clemente's art, which, for all of its introspection and mystical intimations, remains triumphantly and essentially of this world.

Ezra Pound noted that all verse consists of a constant and a variable. In Clemente's work the constant is the human body—the corporeal envelope that we must of necessity inhabit. The variable, then, is all that is extrinsic to this fragile human form. The boundary where these two factors meet—the arena where Clemente's work takes place—determines what one might call *identity*. In a larger sense Clemente's search for identity represents a search for unity, that hoped-for ideal of every philosopher from ancient times to the present. And yet the paradox of this search is that every aspect of our identity is composed of such innumerable elements that the very asking of the question is a plunge into a myriad of forms and meanings as complex as life itself. This is a challenge that Clemente has chosen to meet head on. To find a unity amongst diversity has been his insistent impulse. The lovely evidence of this search has comprised a cosmogony of forms and images so complex and lastingly resonant as to place Clemente alone amongst his contemporaries.

* Robert Creeley, "A Note on the Local," *First Person*, no. 1 (1961); reprinted in Robert Creeley, *The Collected Essays of Robert Creeley* (Berkeley, 1989), p. 479.

15

Italy

Italy

Ann Percy

Naples, where Francesco Clemente was born in 1952 and where he lived until the age of eighteen, is a city of almost indescribable character. "Wedged," in Goethe's phrase, "between God and the Devil,"[1] Naples retains to this day an ancient, dark, and primitive side. Situated in a region of spectacular natural beauty, southern and sunny, blessed with an abundance of growing things, it is in turn crowded, decaying, chaotic, and corrupt. Time and again over the centuries disasters alternatively orchestrated by nature and by man—plagues, earthquakes, famines, revolutions, volcanic eruptions, and wars—have disrupted the life and shaken the ancient fabric of the city. Its oldest history is Greek, and it was a site of importance before the Romans conquered Campania in the fourth century B.C.; even as a dependency of the Roman Republic, Naples clung tenaciously to its Greek character for some time. Situated between the Phlegraean Fields, fertile volcanic site of the region's oldest Greek settlements some six or eight centuries before Christ, and Mount Vesuvius, spectacular instrument of the destruction of Pompeii and Herculaneum in 79 A.D., Naples (or rather the hill of Posilipo overlooking the bay between Naples proper and the ancient town of Pozzuoli) is said to be the site of the tomb of Italy's epic poet Virgil.

Since the end of the Roman Empire, Naples has been ruled by a series of foreign regimes—Gothic, Byzantine, Muslim, Norman, Swabian, Angevin, Aragonese, Spanish, and Austrian—so that the city's history has been a continual layering of diverse cultures over the centuries, and this quality of cultural mingling has proven vital to Clemente's approach to artistic and intellectual issues. Born into an old and aristocratic family, well educated and well traveled as a child, he grew up in the fashionable Chiaia district of Naples and studied classics and Italian literature as a schoolboy. Visually, he was surrounded by the sumptuous—and decaying—Baroque and Rococo churches and palaces of the old city and the paintings, sculptures, and other objects that were created to decorate them.

Clemente, who painted and drew as a child, has often commented that he was exposed to art from an early age. Deep in the crowded, littered, impoverished core of Naples are churches such as San Paolo Maggiore, with its facade that incorporates antique columns from the ruins of the Roman temple upon which it was built; the Gesù Nuovo, with its luminous polychrome marble decoration; and Santa Chiara, with its colorful majolica cloister. The dedicated tourist who makes the effort to explore these neighborhoods finds as well numerous crumbling Baroque and Rococo palaces-turned-tenements, many with the open, soaring double-geometrical staircases that were the particular invention of Ferdinando Sanfelice. In the seventeenth and eighteenth centuries the city also produced a school of painters whose work was as rich and vigorous, brilliant and luminous, as any region in Italy could boast, from the darkly and sensuously naturalistic works of Jusepe de Ribera to the bright, crowded, decorative frescoes and canvases of Luca Giordano, Francesco Solimena, and Francesco de Mura. This was a powerful visual tradition with which to grow up, and Clemente's home contained paintings of the Neapolitan Baroque and Rococo schools, including works attributed to Andrea Vaccaro, Giordano, and Solimena.

Possessed of one of the oldest universities in Europe, established in 1224, Naples has a long and important intellectual history as well, claiming as natives or temporary residents such influential thinkers, writers, poets, and philosophers as Saint Thomas Aquinas, Petrarch, Giovanni Boccaccio, Torquato Tasso, Giordano Bruno, Giambattista Marino, Giambattista Vico, Giacomo Leopardi, and Benedetto Croce. It is to this tradition that Clemente can claim inheritance as a Neapolitan, and of particular importance to him are the writings of the late Renaissance philosopher Giordano Bruno, whose emphasis on a fundamental unity underlying and imparting coherence to the varying and contradictory phenomena of the universe finds a parallel in certain of Clemente's broad theoretical interests. Clemente, in fact, showed a literary bent from his early youth, and when he was twelve his parents arranged for a book of his childhood poems to be published.

Figure 1. Alighiero Boetti (Italian, born 1940)
Map of the World, 1972
Thread on canvas, 61¼ x 93¼" (155.6 x 236.8 cm)
Location unknown

In 1970 Clemente left Naples to study architecture at the University of Rome—an academic interlude that had virtually no effect on his subsequent career—and he began to meet artists and to produce the hundreds of small notational drawings (pp. 26–28, 33, 34) whose images provided the sources for many of his works in later years. His friends in Rome included the conceptual artists Alighiero Boetti and Luigi Ontani, the video and performance artist Joan Jonas, and various film makers and musicians from South America and India. He met his future wife, Alba Primiceri, through his interest in the avant-garde theater, in which she performed. Clemente had become acquainted with contemporary art before his move through the Lucio Amelio gallery, which opened in Naples in 1965 and was soon showing a stimulating selection of international avant-garde work, as well as from his own travels. As he has described, "At sixteen I discovered there were living artists, I saw a show of Twombly's and a film by the Roman artists SMKP2. . . . I got around a lot, I even went to Milan quite a bit and, for better or for worse, between 1968 and 1971 I saw a great deal of art; there were an extraordinary number of shows to see, and I was very curious to see what artists were doing" and "what the artists of the generation before mine were doing."[2]

The most visible members of the artistic generation before Clemente's belonged to the movement known as Arte Povera (literally, "Poor Art"), Italy's major contribution to the conceptual modes of the late 1960s and 1970s. These artists used "poor," unorthodox, or commonplace materials, both natural and industrial, sometimes apparently drawn from the scrap heap—such as dirt, steel, glass, putty, rags, chemicals, neon, water, clay, trees, cotton, wax, butter, ice, and fire—initially as a rejection of consumerism and the marketplace. The artist-alchemist drew upon natural resources such as chemical reactions, the force of gravity, or even live animals, and used them in the creation of works of art. Artists showing from 1967 on under this rubric, the term itself a creation of the Italian critic Germano Celant, included Clemente's friend Boetti and Pino Pascali, whose works particularly affected Clemente in his early years in Rome. Conceptual in nature but not always reductive or demate-rialized in appearance, Arte Povera works generally have a sensuous and highly charged physical presence as individual objects or in the form of actions or installations. The 1968 film that had particularly impressed Clemente, SMKP2, was a "documentary" made by the Duchampian conceptual artist Luca Patella, who occasionally exhibited with the Arte Povera artists in the 1960s and 1970s. It showed activities by Fabio Sargentini, Elisio Mattiacci, Jannis Kounellis, Pascali, and Patella, in which Pascali created a series of actions at the edge of the sea that were based on mythological themes.[3]

In Clemente's beginning years in Rome, Boetti introduced him to the dealer Gian Enzo Sperone, who gave Clemente several of his earliest shows, and furthered his attraction toward the East through the trip to Afghanistan they made together in 1974. Boetti's own work defies categorization and often description; his conceptual pieces frequently involve classifying systems—such as pairing the names of artists of his generation with secret sym-bols or listing the thousand longest rivers in the world in order of size—and often they are executed by someone other than Boetti himself; for example, he had a map embroidered by craftsmen in Afghanistan (Figure 1). The appropriation of traditional workmanship became part of Clemente's method as well, as when he used young Indian craftsmen trained in the Mughal-Rajput tradition of painting to execute his series of Indian miniatures in 1980–81 (pp. 98–109).

In the 1970s the beguiling Luigi Ontani, an older contemporary and friend with whom Cle-mente occasionally exhibited in the late 1970s and early 1980s, was showing photographs of himself in tableaux vivants as various historic or fictional personalities, such as Dracula, Don Quixote, Tarzan, Dante, or David with the head of Goliath. Ontani and Clemente both draw upon a combination of Mediterranean and Indian sources for their imagery, with fre-quent references to figures from classical mythology, Italian history, religion, and legend.

Figure 2. Luigi Ontani (Italian, born 1943)
Untitled
Location unknown

Figure 3. Cy Twombly (American, born 1928)
The Italians, 1961
Oil, pencil, and crayon on canvas; 78⅝ x 102¼"
(199.7 x 259.7 cm)
The Museum of Modern Art, New York.
Blanchette Rockefeller Fund, 504.69

Figure 4. Francesco Clemente
Telamon, 1980
Pastel and charcoal on paper, 80 x 340"
(203.2 x 863.6 cm)
Anthony d'Offay Gallery, London

They also each have worked with photographs and imaginative figurative drawings in which parts of the body metamorphose into fantasy shapes (Figure 2). And, like Clemente and Boetti, Ontani has had work produced to his designs by artisans in other countries.

By the mid-1970s it was clear to Clemente that he could not become a sort of "second-generation" Arte Povera artist. The eclecticism of the movement had opened his mind to a variety of sources that he might not otherwise have encountered, but in the end he saw it, in relation to himself, as creating a vacuum that he felt free to fill, a climate of liberation in which to draw and paint. Clemente's reaction was against both the elaborate theoretical posturings of the 1960s and 1970s and the use of untraditional and unorthodox materials: "There was . . . a great desire to restore reality to what we were doing as artists; whereas somehow all that esoteric and sophistic baggage of the late sixties, of the artists of those years, seemed to have been usurped by the politicians, by the street. It seemed that nothing could be done in that direction."[4] Clemente instead was to move toward the use of a wide range of traditional mediums and materials; toward a reassumption of oil, canvas, watercolor, and pastel; and toward a reaffirmation of the expressive use of the human figure, especially his own.

Clemente's interest in traditional mediums and approaches was in part inspired by the works of the American artist Cy Twombly, a long-time resident of Italy and a generation older than Clemente, who had moved out of Abstract Expressionism to create a unique painterly and calligraphic treatment of picture surfaces: "Looking at those Cy Twombly paintings, I knew that they had a tremendous integrity that wasn't in any of the Arte Povera works. One could say, of course, that [Alberto] Burri's work had the same integrity, but the difference, I think, is that Twombly had a more Mediterranean soul than Burri. . . . There is more joy and more hope and more light, more Italian light, in Twombly's paintings than in Burri's" (Figure 3).[5]

Both Twombly and Clemente are much affected by Italy's ancient past and especially its classical mythology. Both depict or entitle works with antique subjects—philosophers and poets, gods and heroes—or motifs (Figure 4). Clemente has mentioned his liking for certain classical authors—such as Apuleius and Petronius—and periods—in particular late antiquity, the Rome of Hadrian and the Pantheon. As he has said, "The Egyptians, Greeks and Romans are still more alive for me than live people, other painters. . . . I am a link in the long chain with the past."[6] Indeed, in 1979 his contribution to the exhibition *Le Stanze*, held at the Castello Colonna at Genazzano, near Rome, was a floor mosaic of a boy and a fish, whose humorous distortions are modern but whose ultimate ancestry is clearly antique (for the drawing from which the mosaic was derived, see Figure 5). Both Clemente and Twombly combine erudition with emotionalism and use imagery that occasionally is intensely erotic. But whereas the awesome, violent, epic, and chaotic aspects of a dark and primitive past often seem to lie coiled behind Twombly's "antique" subjects, for Clemente the seduction of the classical world appears less epic and usually more comic; for example, in *Not the Death of Heraclitus* of 1980 a monster-infant sprouts mushrooms from his abdomen (Figure 6), and in the pastel *Caduceo* of 1981 Mercury's caduceus becomes a pair of entwined tails, one human, one rodent (p. 75).

Another artist with whom Clemente feels a spiritual affinity is Joseph Beuys, whom he first met in Italy in 1974.[7] Beuys had a special fondness for Naples, where his first Italian show was held in 1971, where he went to give assistance after the devastating earthquake of 1980, and where his last major work, a shamanistic "tomb" that seemingly forecast his own imminent death in 1986, was created and exhibited in 1985. Although the German artist's work is heavily theoretical and symbolic in a way that Clemente's is not, and although the political activism that was so strong a part of Beuys's life and art is not a part of Clemente's, the younger artist responds to an artistic intent he finds in Beuys that seeks to retrieve and revive

Figure 5. Francesco Clemente
Untitled, 1978
Ink on paper, 17 x 9¹/₁₆″ (43.2 x 23 cm)
Öffentliche Kunstsammlung,
Kupferstichkabinett, Basel. 1984.78

Figure 6. Francesco Clemente
Not the Death of Heraclitus, 1980
Pastel and charcoal on three sheets of paper, 79 x 312″
(200.7 x 792.5 cm)
Private Collection, Courtesy Galerie
Bruno Bischofberger, Zurich

Figure 7. Joseph Beuys (German, 1921–1986)
Energy M3, 1971
Pencil on paper, 11³/₄ x 8½″ (29.8 x 21.6 cm)
Anthony d'Offay Gallery, London

lost or forgotten elements of common human experience or consciousness in order to move people away from their material, rational selves and back to their more mystical or spiritual ones. This intent legitimizes for Clemente the reasons for becoming an artist. Both Clemente and Beuys have made use of the medium of drawing as a way of thinking that connects earlier to later works and links all aspects of their *oeuvres*, and both have produced great quantities of drawings, using them as part of a generative process and as a reservoir of basic source material (Figure 7).[8]

Between 1970 and 1980, for example, Clemente—who worked primarily on paper all through the decade—executed several hundred small ink drawings and pastels on irregularly shaped pieces of paper (see pp. 26–28, 33, 34). These depict a variety of images or ideas—such as humans and animals that metamorphose into strange shapes or assemblages of body parts, scarves that turn into hands, and house fronts with noses and mouths—and frequently incorporate words used in a poetic, evocative way. Often scatological and always hallucinogenic, the sheets are like notations or doodles, and for years were simply scattered around the artist's studio in Rome, but they actually constitute for Clemente "an endless stream of images that seemed to generate one another,"[9] "each of which was tied to an idea,"[10] and that provided visual sources for many of his paintings. Although small in scale, these works have a subtle but potent aura through the quality of the drawn line, the bizarreness of the images, and the varied tones and irregular shapes of the sheets of paper. By 1977–78 Clemente had begun to edit, assemble, photograph, and enlarge these drawings to incorporate them in various ways into other works (pp. 35, 36).

Despite the fact that he was producing hundreds of small drawn images in the 1970s, when Clemente first began to exhibit in the early years of the decade his pieces most resembled those of the American language artists Joseph Kosuth, Douglas Huebler, Robert Barry, and Lawrence Weiner, who were then showing with the same galleries as Clemente: Gian Enzo Sperone in Rome and Turin and Franco Toselli in Milan. In an effort to close the gap between idea and materials, language and image, these artists were using written texts, sometimes combined with drawings or photographs (Figure 8). Although their approaches were highly theoretical in a way that his was not, Clemente similarly used or combined written or typed words, photographs, and slide projections (Figure 9), a mode he shared with many other Italian conceptual artists working at the time.[11]

Among the other Italian conceptual artists who were important for Clemente at this period was the remarkable Piero Manzoni, dead in 1963 at the age of thirty, who had produced conceptual works with a sort of Duchampian wit and purity in the late 1950s and early 1960s that anticipate by several years the earth, body, performance, and process art of the late 1960s. In his attempt to free art from concerns of color, shape, symbol, and allegory and to equate art with the human body and life, Manzoni eliminated color from his canvases and added unconventional materials such as cotton wool or bread rolls to their surfaces; projected the packaging and sale of balloons of "artist's breath"; drew long lines (of up to four and a half miles) on rolls of paper that he placed in sealed containers; made a "magic base" with footprints on top (anyone is a work of art who stands on it); and produced and tinned ninety cans of "artist's shit."[12] His brief career was highly influential in the decade following his early death. Clemente was impressed by the way in which Manzoni combined a conceptual intention with very strong visual imagery, a characteristic that also describes much of Clemente's work of the mid-1970s. He was also attracted at that time to the work of Vincenzo Agnetti, an older figure who was one of Italy's most important conceptual artists and a close collaborator of Manzoni. Also a critic and essayist, Agnetti was concerned with language, its relativity, ambiguity, and ultimate obscurity; like many conceptual artists, he presented his analyses in the form of words, photographs, and occasionally recordings, or a combination thereof.

Figure 8. Douglas Huebler (American, born 1924)
Variable Piece No. 70 (in Process), 1976
Typed statement and color photographs
mounted on paper; left: 28¼ x 36⅛" (71.7 x 91.8 cm),
right: 28¼ x 28¼" (71.7 x 71.7 cm)
Location unknown

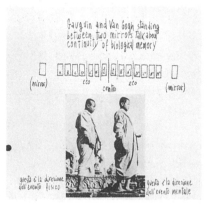

Figure 9. Francesco Clemente
On the Continuity of Biological Memory, 1973,
from Museum of the Philadelphia Civic Center,
Italy Two: Art Around '70
(November 2–December 16, 1973)

Figure 10. Francesco Clemente
Progetto per un grattacielo in vetro (1921), from *Pierre Menard* (Rome: Edizioni GAP, 1973)

Between 1973 and 1976 Clemente was at his most conceptual, combining words and photographic imagery or using typed statements on sheets of paper. His *Pierre Menard* of 1973 (Figure 10), for example, is an exercise in ambiguity, a small book of manipulated photographs of well-known modern buildings by architects such as Frank Lloyd Wright, Le Corbusier, Walter Gropius, and Louis Kahn, with some element altered to introduce small errors in proportions or details. The title refers to a short story by Jorge Luis Borges about a Pierre Menard, who undertakes to write a portion of *Don Quixote*, not intending to copy it but "to produce a few pages which would coincide—word for word and line for line—with those of Miguel de Cervantes,"[13] a deliberate anachronism in which Menard seeks to arrive at the *Quixote* through his own experience. During these years Clemente also began to make diptychs of photographs of pieces of fabric in gridlike serial arrangements (Figure 11), which he characterized as male or female according to the pattern (for example, the rigid intersecting lines of plaid were male, while softer floral patterns were female). He also combined framed photographs with semisculptural objects or placed them as stacks on the floor, as in *The Little House of Morals*, shown in 1973.[14] In 1974 he began to do photographic pieces consisting of numerous similarly or identically patterned images, such as tea leaves, birds in flight, or floor tiles, that he framed separately and hung in serial progression in a variety of configurations (cross-shaped, T-shaped, or asymmetrical), occasionally consuming the entire length of a gallery wall (p. 30). For example, *A Place Without an Enemy* (p. 30) consists of framed photographs of slides of Clemente's drawings projected on the walls of a gallery in Rome interspersed with photographs of geometrical images; *Teas* (p. 29), of twelve photographs of tea leaves that can be hung in different framed configurations; and *Le Pazienze* (Figure 12), of seven color photographs of various types of seeds in which the image functions as the frame and empty space is at the center. However much Clemente may have been playing with ideas in these pieces, they are all strongly visual, and he continued to draw on both a smaller and larger scale throughout this period.[15] Underlying his conceptual works are an intentional ambiguity, a lack of dogmatism, and an enigmatic wish to present an appearance of order, the key to which does not exist. Rather than following a clear-cut conceptual process to arrive at a certain image, he sought to create a distance between the endless flux of his drawn images and the boundary line of the frame, which isolates the individual one and makes it readable.

By 1978, still living in Italy but feeling the impact of his fourth and longest-yet stay in India that year, Clemente had moved into a predominantly figural mode of expression, producing large, colorful gouaches of bizarrely juxtaposed images against empty or patterned grounds. Applying the label "figurative" to Clemente's works is, however, misleading, for despite his almost exclusive concentration on the human body after the late 1970s, he does not consider himself a figurative painter. With their often-blurred lines of distinction between abstraction and corporeality, his depictions of the human body resonate between intensities of the cerebral and the sensual. In his large gouaches of 1978–80 disembodied hands fling small images of famous buildings up against blank spaces spangled with galaxies of rings (p. 38); or a ship sails through dense blackness surrounded by moonlike portholes filled with rats, bananas, noses, and bottles (p. 40); or naked men assume dancelike positions while attached to wild animals flying off into space (p. 39).

Bridging the space between these imagist works and the earlier conceptual ones are *Whether the Holes in the Body Are Nine or Ten* of 1977 (p. 35), in which ten drawings on cloud-shaped pieces of torn cardboard surround greatly enlarged photographs of one of the small notational drawings, and *Harlequin Close Up* of 1978 (p. 36), in which nine of the small notational drawings are mounted on linen. In these years Clemente was still producing installations that combined drawings and objects, such as *Undae clemente flamina pulsae*, in which color photographs of Indian kitsch sculpture, paintings on sheets of metal, color photo-

Figure 11. Francesco Clemente
Portrait: Male and Female, 1974
Eighteen photographs, approximately 11 x 22″
(27.9 x 55.9 cm) (overall)
Location unknown

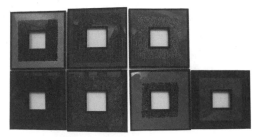

Figure 12. Francesco Clemente
Le Pazienze, 1974
Seven color photographs, each approximately 15 x 15″
(38.1 x 38.1 cm)
Private Collection

Figure 13. Francesco Clemente
Undae clemente flamina pulsae, 1978
Mixed-media installation
Groninger Museum, Groningen, The Netherlands.
1980–490

graphs of such paintings, and retouched photographs of everyday objects were all assembled on a wall (Figure 13). This piece was commemorated in a small book printed in India (see Figure 16). In 1978 Clemente began to explore his special affinity for the self-portrait in a series of large, loosely and calligraphically rendered Chinese ink, pastel, and gouache drawings of himself, usually nude, each with a strange accouterment, disruption, truncation, juxtaposition, or metamorphosis. Birds, for example, crowd upon the shoulders of the staring Clemente (p. 41), or his arms, legs, and head reverse their positions (p. 42), or he appears, in the end, as a garden (p. 69).

Among the most "Italian" of all Clemente's works are a group of oil, pastel, or charcoal pieces produced in 1980, not long before he left Italy as a permanent residence, that share a quality of reference to classical subject matter, to medieval manuscripts, or to Renaissance emblem books. Each of the series of drawings entitled *Codex* (pp. 45–47) evokes the format of a manuscript volume opened to a single- or double-page spread, while in *Fortune and Virtue* (p. 44) and *Waning Moon* (Figure 14), Clemente uses block lettering that suggests ancient Roman inscriptions as well as emblematic references to abstract qualities such as fortune or virtue. Among his huge pastel and charcoal drawings, *Telamon* (Figure 4) depicts male figures used to support entablatures or cornices in classical architecture, and *Not the Death of Heraclitus* (Figure 6) refers to the Greek philosopher who taught that eternal change is the only actuality and that unity lies in diversity and multiplicity, ideas that Clemente's own intellectual searchings reflect.

In this move away from a conceptual mode of working, the qualities of enigma and ambiguity that had characterized Clemente's early pieces continued to inform his mature ones. In this he remains particularly affected by an earlier generation of Italian painters, among them the metaphysical and proto-Surrealist painter Giorgio de Chirico and other artists of his circle working in the period between the two world wars, such as de Chirico's brother Alberto Savinio and their slightly younger contemporary Filippo de Pisis. Clemente has cited de Chirico's prayer of the artist to God — "Please let me be able to give again to art, to painting, the dignity of two centuries ago"[16] — and compared Savinio's writing process, in which the same subjects are combined in different ways using a variety of labyrinthine shifts and turns ("In this flow, extremely original and unique things come out"), to his own approach to art.[17] In de Pisis he finds a sort of ironic detachment that eliminates the differences between the weak and the strong, the ugly and the beautiful, rendering the work a continuous flow in which each element has the same weight.[18] Several characteristics of the so-called Metaphysical School of painting, which asserted the fantastic and enigmatic in art, and which grew particularly out of the interaction of de Chirico, Savinio, de Pisis, and Carlo Carrà during the First World War, are similar to Clemente's pictorial approach.

Savinio is better known as a writer, composer, and stage and set designer than as a painter. "His painting emerged from literature and later returned to its literary origins; his music is a form of ballet which aspires to pure imagery in motion; his stage designs — which complete the cycle — can be viewed as painting, which in turn undergoes a metamorphosis into literary discourse."[19] This seeking to merge literary and visual expression is characteristic of Clemente as well. He is deeply interested in literature (that of England and the United States as well as of his own country), wrote poetry as a child, and draws from certain writers' modes of literary composition in forming his own working methods. He is particularly attracted to Savinio's writings and in 1983–86 illustrated one of his major books, *The Departure of the Argonaut* (p. 178 and Figure 54). Especially notable is the parallel between de Chirico's and Savinio's penchant for combining references to mythology or classical antiquity with contemporary, personal, everyday, and even kitsch motifs (Figure 15), and Clemente's own interweaving of the commonplace with literary or classical allusions (pp. 44, 75, 130, and

Figure 14. Francesco Clemente
Waning Moon, 1980
Oil on paper, mounted on linen; 59 x 108"
(149.9 x 274.3 cm)
Courtesy Thomas Ammann, Zurich

Figure 15. Giorgio de Chirico (Italian, 1888–1978)
The Transformed Dream, 1913
Oil on canvas, 24¾ x 59⅞" (62.9 x 152.1 cm)
The Saint Louis Art Museum. Anonymous Gift,
313:1951

Figure 6).[20] The telescoping of elements from past and present time, strange metamorphoses from human to animal or animate to inanimate, abrupt disruptions in scale, disjunctions between interior and exterior spaces, and the juxtaposition of often bizarrely disparate elements are characteristic of de Chirico, Savinio, and Clemente.

Clemente responds to this quality of enigma in de Chirico's and Savinio's work as well as to the brothers' nostalgia for regional or local flavor. Their cultivated, worldly, polyglot background—schooled in Athens and Munich, resident in Paris, Milan, and Florence—likewise appeals to the younger artist. Part of this attraction, for Clemente, is to the memory of a vanished world, to a lost high bourgeois as well as a provincial Italian culture:

> *I think it was Savinio who wrote of Europe and of the European middle class before the First World War, saying that we'll never be able to imagine what Europe was like then. I feel those very good years from 1913 to 1918 were largely a result of the disappearance of a way of life or a class in Europe that left these survivors, the painters, who found themselves suspended in a void and had to create a new world to replace the world that no longer was. The same thing has happened in Europe in recent years, I think. The artists have passed through at least one war; and for the first time each one of them, from Enzo Cucchi to Anselm Kiefer, has succeeded in sinking his roots into the soil of his own birthplace, just at the moment when ethnic differences were wiped out, as in the last ten years. We've seen it happen in Italy: when everything that was pleasant and local had been leveled, a painter like Enzo—the painter of the Marches, the eternal periphery of a world that has become totally peripheral—came along.*[21]

This loss of regional character in Italy lamented by Clemente had its origins in economic, political, and social changes following the Second World War that culminated in the events of the late 1960s. In Italy, as in the United States and France, 1968 was a year of student demonstrations, which quickly spread to the Italian factories and unions. During the riots in the summer of 1968 students occupied the Accademia delle Belle Arti in Venice and disrupted the Biennale, one of the major international art exhibitions, partly to protest the latter's policies and selection methods and partly to voice their dissatisfaction with the art establishment in general. The next year was marked by more strikes and student riots, and by the outbreak of urban terrorism. The 1970s in Italy was a decade of economic recession, inflation, unemployment, student riots, and terrorist kidnappings and bombings, as well as major social changes such as the legalization of divorce. Whereas Clemente was not militant he was sympathetic to the student protests, and he shared in his generation's post-1968 sentiment of disaffection and skepticism toward Italian life in general. In particular he regretted the loss of "innocence" Italy suffered in the 1970s as a result of the radical and liberal battles over such issues as abortion, divorce, gay rights, and feminism.[22] He saw the Italian working class becoming integrated into a sort of general European bourgeoisie, with the differences that give the country its national character rapidly disappearing. He also did not want to deal further with the weight of his own tradition, with a legacy of "great but half-dead ideas," as he has put it.[23] By the late 1970s all these factors had combined to encourage him to move elsewhere.

Clemente was looking both east—to India—and west—to New York—in his search for a new mode of artistic expression. Of his various trips to India in the 1970s, his extended stays in 1977 and 1978 had proven especially catalytic for his art. Virtually all of his work on paper after 1980 has been created in the United States or in India, with the exception of a number of prints he made with the printer-publisher Walter Rossi in Rome in the late 1980s. In 1981 Clemente produced his first group of prints, at Crown Point Press in San Francisco (pp. 129–32), and in 1982 he settled permanently in New York. By this time his work was reaching its full expressive range in media and technique—ink drawings, gouaches, charcoals, pastels, watercolors, frescoes, oils, books, etchings, and aquatints — and he had enlarged the scale of his works on paper to equal that of sizable paintings by joining multiple sheets of handmade Indian paper with strips of cotton (pp. 70–73). Moving away from the spare, language-oriented conceptual art of his beginnings, he had reassumed the commitment of the art-historical past to traditional techniques of drawing, painting, and printmaking and to figurative subject matter, and with these tools he has generated a remarkable and unique body of images. This is not to say that major Italian influences do not linger or that Clemente does not return often to Italy, which he does both for family reasons and for the chance to create certain works, particularly frescoes, with the craftsmen and materials that he finds there. His trips to India in 1977–78 marked the end of his "Italian" period, however, and the dialogue of the 1980s and 1990s is no longer an Italian but an American one.

1. J. W. Goethe, *Italian Journey (1786–1788)*, trans. W. H. Auden and Elizabeth Mayer (San Francisco, 1982), p. 207.
2. Quoted in Giancarlo Politi, "Francesco Clemente," *FlashArt*, no. 117 (April–May 1984), pp. 18–19.
3. Tommaso Trini, "The Sixties in Italy," *Studio International*, vol. 184, no. 949 (November 1972), pp. 168–69; and Germano Celant, *Identité italienne: L'art en Italie depuis 1959* (Paris, 1981), pp. 275, 279.
4. Clemente as quoted in Politi, "Clemente," p. 16.
5. Quoted in Rainer Crone and Georgia Marsh, *Clemente: An Interview with Francesco Clemente* (New York, 1987), p. 17.
6. Quoted in Paul Gardner, "Gargoyles, Goddesses and Faces in the Crowd," *ARTnews*, vol. 85, no. 3 (March 1985), p. 58.
7. Dieter Koepplin, *Francesco Clemente CVIII: Watercolours Adayar 1985* (Zurich, 1987), p. 16 n. 13 (English text, Zurich, 1988, p. 11).
8. As Beuys said of his drawings, "I ask questions, I put forms of language on paper, I also put forms of sensibility, intention and idea on paper, all in order to stimulate thought. . . . My drawings make a kind of reservoir for me, that I can get important impulses from. In other words, they're a kind of basic source material that I can draw from again and again." Quoted in conversation with Heiner Bastian and Jeannot Simmen, in Museum Boymans–Van Beuningen, Rotterdam, *Joseph Beuys: Zeichnungen/Tekeningen/Drawings* (November 1979–January 1980), p. 94.
9. Clemente as quoted in Crone and Marsh, *Clemente*, p. 25.
10. Clemente as quoted in Politi, "Clemente," p. 15.
11. For examples of some of this work see the catalogue of the exhibition *Italy Two: Art Around '70*, held at the Museum of the Philadelphia Civic Center (November 2–December 16, 1973); see also Achille Bonito Oliva, *Drawing/Transparence; Disegno/trasparenza* (Rome, 1976). Clemente's most purely verbal piece, consisting of pages of typed text with small photographs paperclipped to them, is reproduced in *FlashArt* (Milan), nos. 46–47 (June 1974), pp. 15–18.
12. See The Tate Gallery, London, *Piero Manzoni: Paintings, Reliefs & Objects* (March 20–May 15, 1974).
13. Jorge Luis Borges, "Pierre Menard, Author of the Quixote," in Jorge Luis Borges, *Labyrinths: Selected Stories and Other Writings*, ed. Donald A. Yates and James E. Irby (Harmondsworth, England, 1970), p. 66.
14. *Francesco Clemente: Gratis* (Geneva, 1978), pl. IV.

15. For reproductions of these early works by Clemente see Giorgio Cortenova, *Empirica: L'arte tra addizione e sottrazione* (1975 [published in conjunction with an exhibition organized by the Comune of Rimini and the Museo Castelvecchio of Verona]), pp. 134–35; Achille Bonito Oliva, "Process, Concept and Behaviour in Italian Art," *Studio International*, vol. 191, no. 979 (January–February 1976), p. 10; Oliva, *Drawing/Transparence;* "Presentazione: Francesco Clemente," *Domus*, no. 577 (December 1977), pp. 52–54; Musée d'Art Moderne de la Ville de Paris, Palais de Tokyo, *10ᵉ Biennale de Paris: Manifestation internationale des jeunes artistes* (September 17–November 1, 1977), pp. 104–5; *Clemente: Gratis*; Achille Bonito Oliva, *Francesco Clemente: Vetta* (Modena, 1979); Gian Enzo Sperone, Turin, *Francesco Clemente: Non scopa* (December 1979); Wolfgang Max Faust, Margarethe Jochimsen, and Achille Bonito Oliva, *Die enthauptete Hand — 100 Zeichnungen aus Italien — Chia, Clemente, Cucchi, Paladino* (Bonn, 1980), pp. 26–50; Mannheimer Kunstverein, *Egomanigativo: Sandro Chia, Francesco Clemente, Nicola de Maria, Mimmo Paladino* (March 30–April 27, 1980); Achille Bonito Oliva, *The Italian Trans-Avantgarde* (Milan, 1980); and Paul Maenz, *Francesco Clemente: "il viaggiatore napoletano"* (Cologne, 1982).
16. Clemente as quoted in Robin White, "Francesco Clemente," *View*, vol. 3, no. 6 (November 1981), p. 2.
17. Ibid., p. 6.
18. Ibid., p. 11.
19. Maurizio Fagiolo dell'Arco, "Biographical Notes on a Metaphysical Argonaut — Alberto Savinio," *Artforum*, vol. 21, no. 5 (January 1983), p. 47.
20. It was Savinio who remarked that "the soul of ancient Greece is no longer to be found in books, but in a bootjack in the form of a lyre" (Paolo Baldacci, "De Chirico and Savinio: The Theory and Iconography of Metaphysical Painting," in Emily Braun, ed., *Italian Art in the 20th Century: Painting and Sculpture, 1900–1988* [London, 1989], p. 70).
21. Clemente as quoted in Politi, "Clemente," pp. 15–16.
22. Clemente as quoted in Crone and Marsh, *Clemente*, p. 14.
23. Quoted in conversation with the author, January 1990.

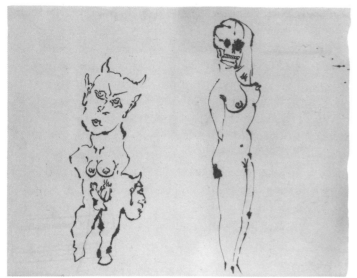

Untitled, 1971
Ink on paper
8⅝ x 11¼″ (21.9 x 28.6 cm)
Öffentliche Kunstsammlung,
Kupferstichkabinett, Basel. 1984.18

Untitled, 1971
Ink on paper
8⅝ x 11⅞″ (21.9 x 30.2 cm)
Öffentliche Kunstsammlung,
Kupferstichkabinett, Basel. 1984.20

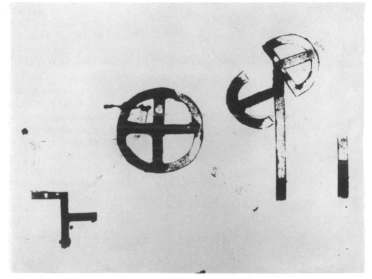

Untitled, 1971
Ink on paper
4¾ x 6¾″ (12.1 x 17.2 cm)
Öffentliche Kunstsammlung,
Kupferstichkabinett, Basel. 1984.22

Untitled, 1971
Ink on paper
8⅝ x 11⅜″ (21.9 x 28.9 cm)
Collection of Francesco and Alba Clemente,
New York

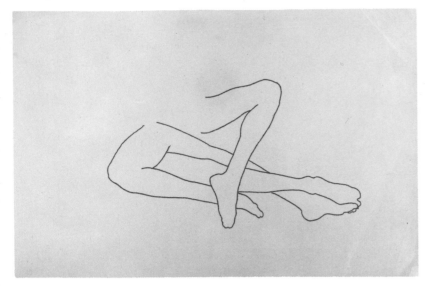

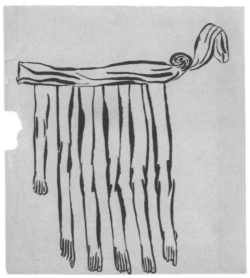

Untitled, 1971
Ink on paper
8⅝ x 13″ (21.9 x 33 cm)
Collection of Francesco and Alba Clemente,
New York

Untitled, 1972
Ink on paper
9¾ x 8⅝″ (24.8 x 21.9 cm)
Öffentliche Kunstsammlung,
Kupferstichkabinett, Basel. 1984.26

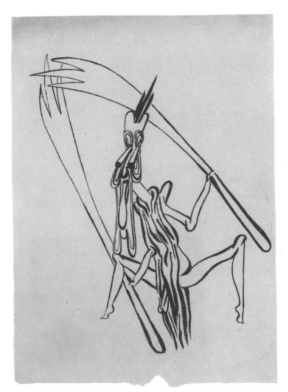

Untitled, 1972
Ink on paper
9⅜ x 5½″ (23.8 x 14 cm)
Öffentliche Kunstsammlung,
Kupferstichkabinett, Basel. 1984.27

Untitled, 1972
Ink on paper
12⅜ x 8⅝″ (31.4 x 21.9 cm)
Öffentliche Kunstsammlung,
Kupferstichkabinett, Basel. 1984.29

Untitled, 1973
Ink and pastel on paper
11½ x 8¾" (29.2 x 22.2 cm)
Öffentliche Kunstsammlung,
Kupferstichkabinett, Basel. 1984.8

Untitled, 1974
Ink on paper
11⅜ x 8⅝" (28.9 x 21.9 cm)
Öffentliche Kunstsammlung,
Kupferstichkabinett, Basel. 1984.51

Untitled, 1975
Ink on paper
12¾ x 8⅝" (32.4 x 21.9 cm)
Öffentliche Kunstsammlung,
Kupferstichkabinett, Basel. 1984.53

Untitled, 1975
Ink on paper
12¾ x 8⅝" (32.4 x 21.9 cm)
Öffentliche Kunstsammlung,
Kupferstichkabinett, Basel. 1984.54

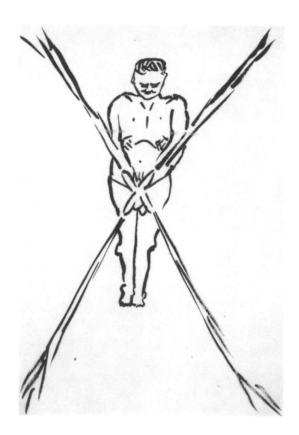

Teas, 1975
Twelve photographs
each 15¾ x 15¾" (40 x 40 cm)
Collection of Francesco and Alba Clemente,
New York

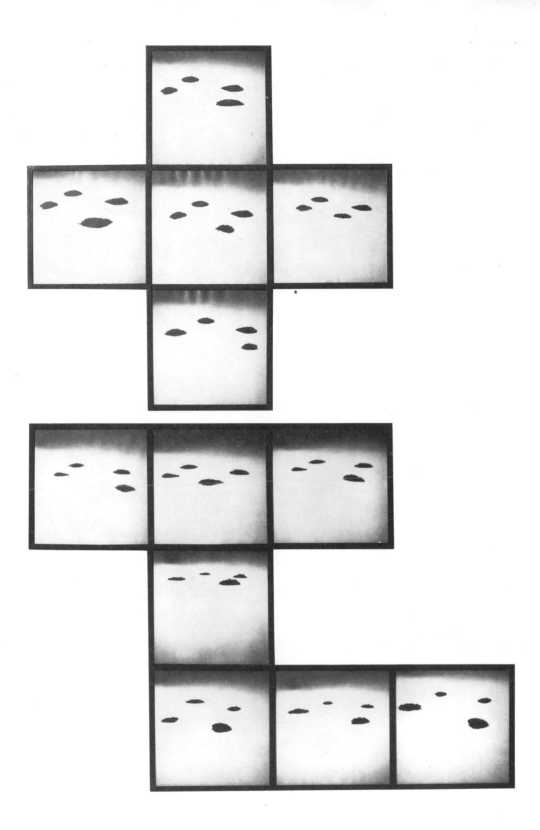

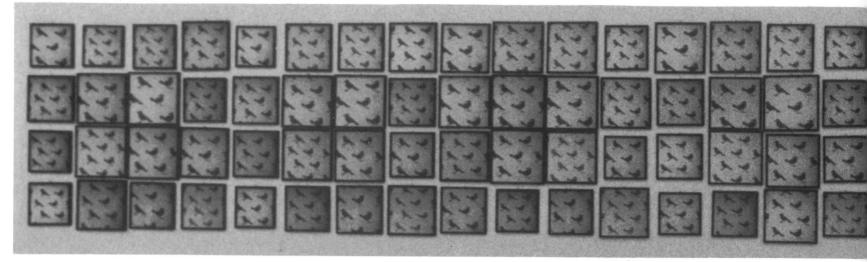

Decorative Motif, 1974
128 photographs
each approximately 8 x 8″ (20.3 x 20.3 cm)
Collection of Marcello Pepori, Arosio, Italy

A Place Without an Enemy, 1975
Eleven photographs
9 x 9″ (22.9 x 22.9 cm) to 12 x 12″
(30.5 x 30.5 cm)
Art & Project, Slootdorp, The Netherlands

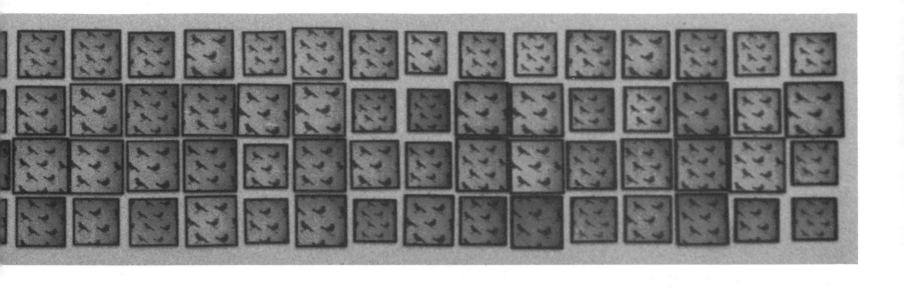

Remainder, 1976
Five photographs
each 7⅞ x 7⅞" (20 x 20 cm)
Collection Sanders, Amsterdam

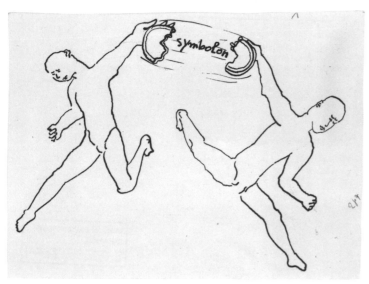

Untitled, 1977
Ink on paper
6¹⁄₈ x 8¼″ (15.6 x 21 cm)
Öffentliche Kunstsammlung,
Kupferstichkabinett, Basel. 1984.60

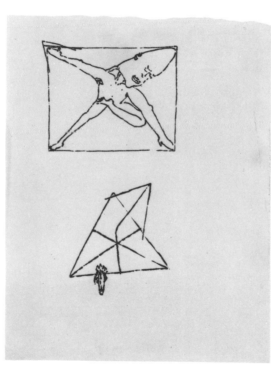

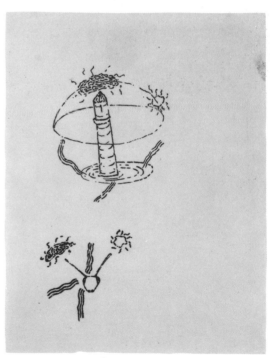

Untitled, 1977
Ink on paper
9¼ x 5¾″ (23.5 x 14.6 cm)
Öffentliche Kunstsammlung,
Kupferstichkabinett, Basel. 1984.62

Untitled, 1977
Ink on paper
11³⁄₈ x 8⁵⁄₈″ (28.9 x 21.9 cm)
Öffentliche Kunstsammlung,
Kupferstichkabinett, Basel. 1984.72

Untitled, 1977
Ink on paper
11⁵⁄₈ x 8⁵⁄₈″ (29.5 x 21.9 cm)
Öffentliche Kunstsammlung,
Kupferstichkabinett, Basel. 1984.73

Untitled, 1977
Watercolor on paper
12⅞ x 8⅝″ (32.7 x 21.9 cm)
Öffentliche Kunstsammlung,
Kupferstichkabinett, Basel. 1984.76

Untitled, 1977
Ink on paper
9¼ x 5¹³/₁₆″ (23.5 x 14.8 cm)
Collection of Francesco and Alba Clemente,
New York

Untitled, 1978
Ink on paper
9 x 8½″ (22.9 x 21.6 cm)
Öffentliche Kunstsammlung,
Kupferstichkabinett, Basel. 1984.80

Untitled, 1977
Ink on paper
5½ x 6¾″ (14 x 17.2 cm)
Öffentliche Kunstsammlung,
Kupferstichkabinett, Basel. 1984.59

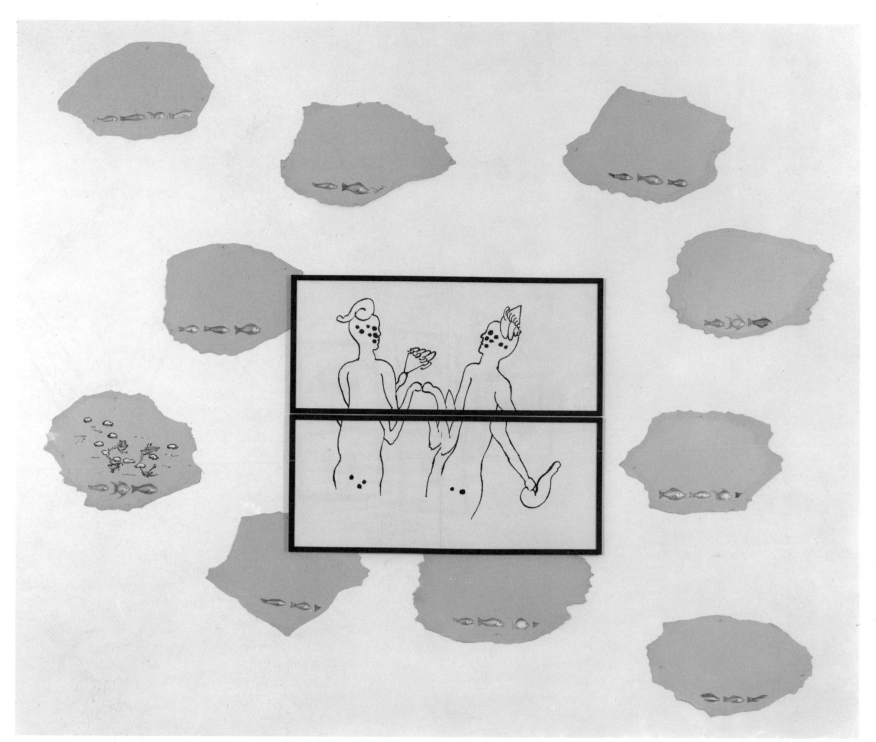

Whether the Holes in the Body Are Nine or Ten, 1977
Enlarged photographs of a drawing framed in
two sections, surrounded by ten drawings
in ink and pastel on cardboard
approximately 96 x 108″ (243.8 x 274.3 cm)
(overall)
Collection of Wolfgang Max Faust, Berlin

35   Italy

Twins, 1978
Ink, gouache, and colored pencil on four sheets
of paper, mounted on linen
93 x 59″ (236.2 x 149.9 cm)
Collection Sanders, Amsterdam

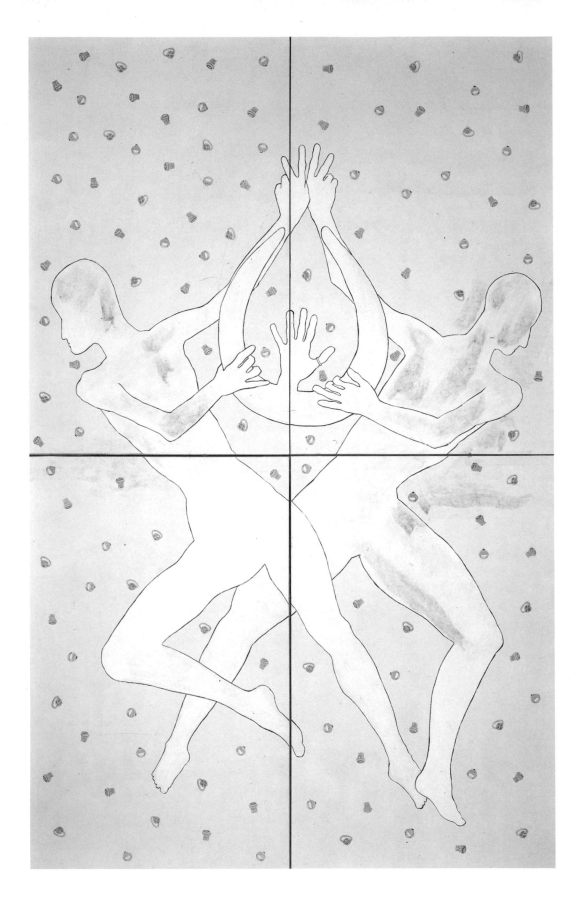

Roma/Milano, 1978–79
Pencil, watercolor, and gouache on paper,
mounted on linen
60¾ x 84¾" (154.3 x 215.3 cm)
Collection Mis, Brussels

Bestiary, 1978
Gouache on paper, mounted on linen
79 x 83″ (200.7 x 210.8 cm)
Private Collection, Courtesy Galerie Bruno
Bischofberger, Zurich

Emblems, 1978
Gouache, chalk, and metallic paint on paper,
mounted on linen
78¼ x 60″ (198.8 x 152.4 cm)
Anthony d'Offay Gallery, London

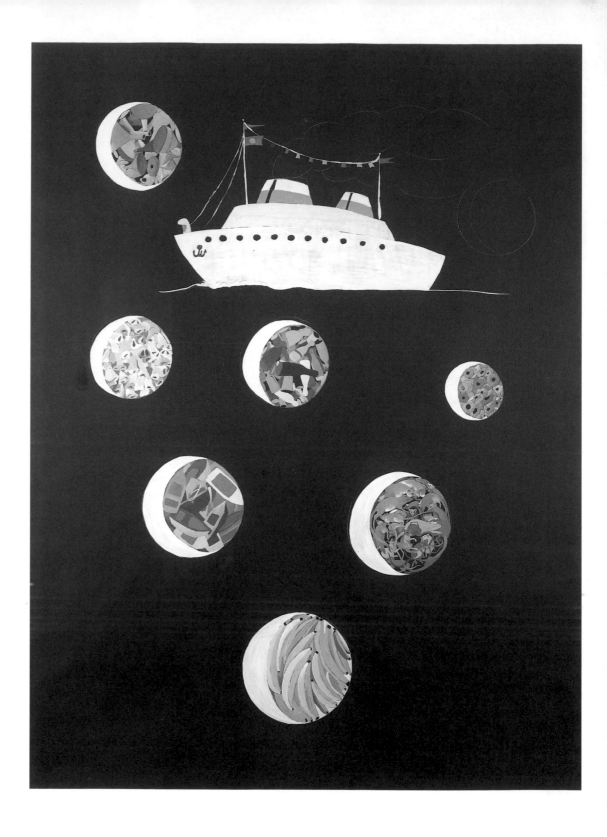

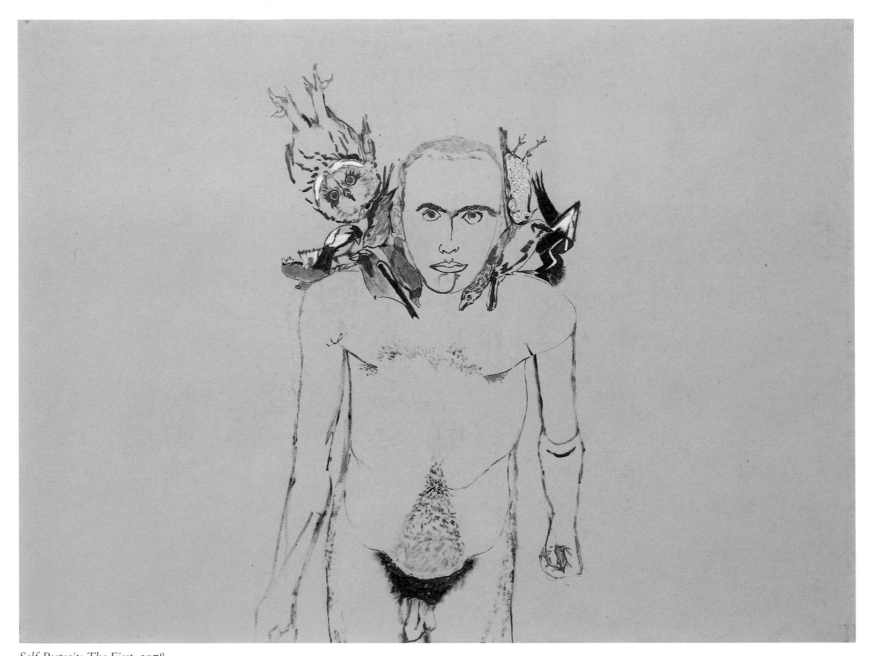

Self-Portrait: The First, 1978
Chinese ink, pastel, and gouache on paper,
mounted on linen
44 x 58" (111.8 x 147.3 cm)
Private Collection, Courtesy Galerie Bruno
Bischofberger, Zurich

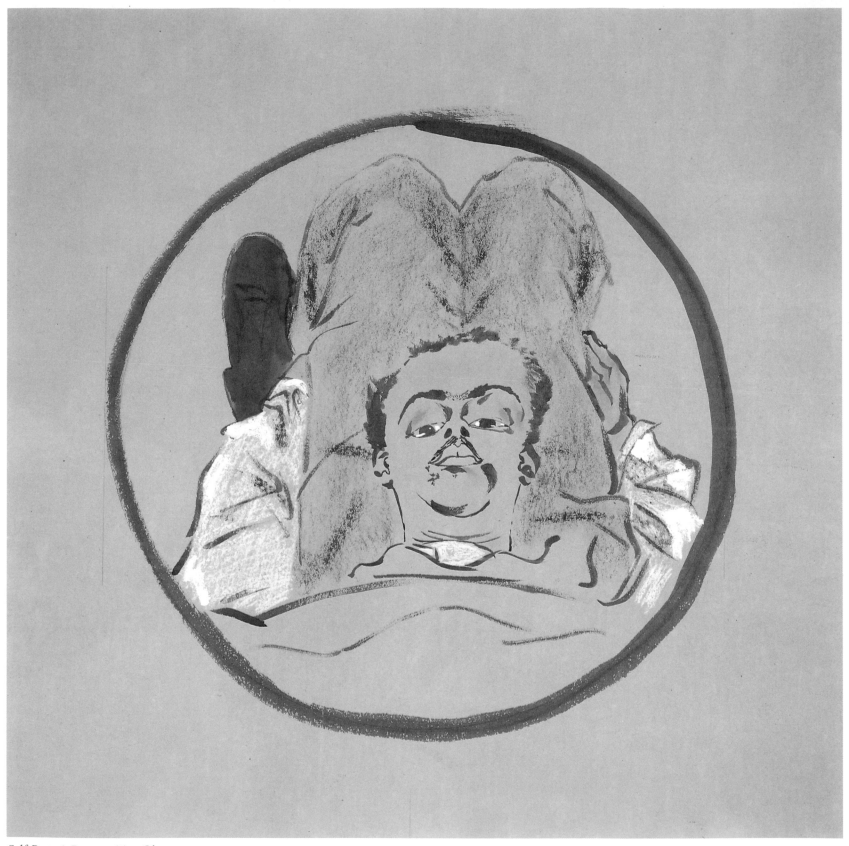

Self-Portrait Between Two Glances, 1979
Chinese ink, pastel, pencil, and gouache
on paper, mounted on linen
39¼ x 39⅜" (99.7 x 100 cm)
Private Collection, Courtesy Galerie Bruno
Bischofberger, Zurich

Self-Portrait Without a Broom, 1979
Chinese ink and gouache on paper,
mounted on linen
83¹/₂ x 128″ (212.1 x 325.1 cm)
Private Collection, Courtesy Galerie Bruno
Bischofberger, Zurich

Fortune and Virtue, 1980
Oil, pencil, and pastel on paper,
mounted on linen
59 x 108″ (149.9 x 274.3 cm)
Courtesy Thomas Ammann, Zurich

Codex, 1980
Series of eleven drawings in pastel on paper
each 18 x 24″ (45.7 x 61 cm)
Collection of Francesco and Alba Clemente,
New York (1, 3–11); Collection of Henry
Geldzahler, New York (2)

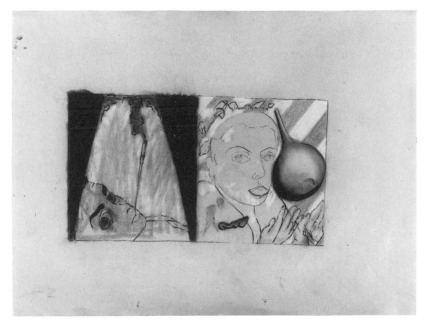

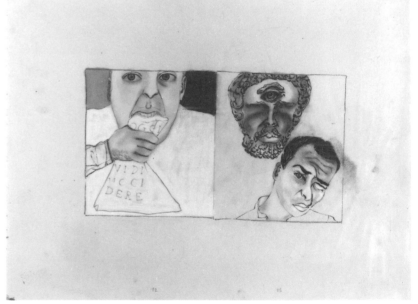

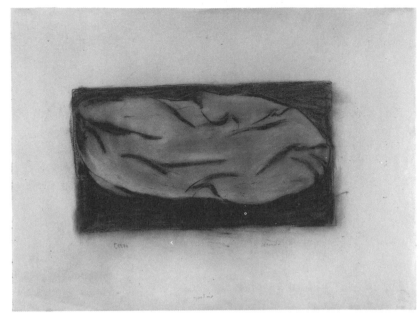

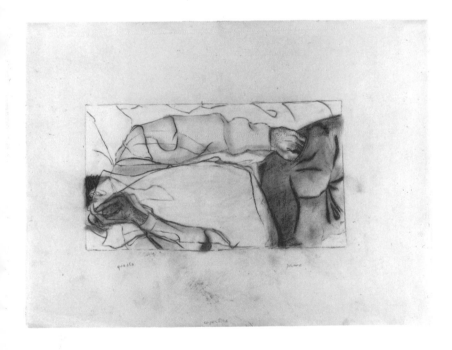

Madras

Madras

Madras

Raymond Foye

"What unifies is what you don't know," Clemente once said. "I am always more interested in what I don't know than what I know."[1] Clemente's comment bears an uncanny echoing of the opening lines of the *Kena Upanishads:* "It is not understood by those who understand it; it is understood by those who do not understand it."[2] It is an instinctive anathema to anyone trained in the ways of Western logic to consider wisdom as the domain of the incognizant. But it is precisely in the state of unknowing, outside of intellect and the five senses, that we apprehend the ultimate reality that is the aim of enlightenment. This is a fundamental truth of the mystical tradition, a tradition of which Clemente's work partakes and from which it in part derives. It is dangerous if not impossible to demark the differences between the "East" and the "West," and Clemente has often stated that such artificially contrived terms have no meaning for him. But if such a line can be drawn, surely it lies in the distinction between vision (West) and insight (East), with vision defined as the purely rational, outward gaze of the objective mind, seeking to know that which is perceived; and insight defined as the mind turned in upon itself, seeking to know that which is perceiving. If the physical fact of Clemente's work is determined by the common boundaries of the intrinsic and extrinsic worlds, the visual content of his work is suspended between the poles of vision and insight.

For an artist who spent the first twenty years of his life in the grip of Roman Catholicism, India became a link with the pagan past of southern Italy, a past that had been nearly obliterated by the church but that lingered on in myriad symbols and myths. "The gods who left us thousands of years ago in Naples are still in India, so it's like going home for me. In India, I can feel what it was like [in Italy] many years ago."[3] Clemente's observation is a striking one in that it conveys an entirely unexpected jolt of recognition, a firsthand discovery that ours is an Indo-European tradition. For Clemente the result was a living restoration of ideas and values that had previously existed only as historical notion.

Clemente's first trip to India was in 1973. India loomed large over the cultural landscape of the 1960s, when its music, art, and religions were simplistically popularized and often vulgarized. Nevertheless the culture and mystical traditions of India found fertile soil in the counterculture movement in the West, and Clemente's first visit was essentially in response to these circumstances. He had been influenced by a friend in Rome who had traveled in India and returned with stories that sparked his imagination. This same friend lent Clemente a book of discussions with a holy man in Delhi, R. P. Kaushik, a homeopathic doctor and former political militant. Like many Indians of his generation, Kaushik had been greatly influenced by the influx of young people from the West, and his teachings fused radical Western notions of politics and personal liberation with traditional aspects of Indian thought. His ideas presented Clemente with the hope of finding a way out of the closure of purely political thinking, into a more basic sense of personal integrity and responsibility deriving from one's own experience. The attraction of these dialogues, combined with the artist's restlessness and boredom with the status quo in Rome (where he had moved from Naples in 1970), cemented his decision to leave Italy. "I wanted to be somewhere else," Clemente said flatly, years later, "and I thought that was as far as I could go and I had the surprise of my life. I mean, I just couldn't believe my eyes."[4]

Overwhelmed by the poverty and the bewildering array of people, customs, and religions in India, Clemente's romantic or sentimental ideas about that country quickly fell away. Roused from the spiritual lethargy of his life in Rome, he now found unfathomable India a challenge to everything he knew. Having lost all sense of time, place, or identity, and faced with this seemingly limitless diversity, Clemente eventually chose to embrace his disorientation: "I was really attracted to [India] . . . by the fact that I didn't understand it. It was my own incomprehension that was alluring."[5]

If what initially attracted Clemente to India was its dissimilarity to the West, what kept him intrigued was the correspondence between the two. The three months Clemente lived in

Figure 16. Plate from Francesco Clemente, *Undae clemente flamina pulsae* (Amsterdam: Art & Project, 1978)

India, in 1973, were largely spent in an ashram in Delhi, listening to dialogues between Kaushik and his four students, two Indians and two Europeans. It was during this first visit that Clemente discovered that the venerable tradition of oral transmission, valued in the days of the pre-Socratic philosophers but now lost to the West, remained very much alive in India. It was, in Clemente's words, "an oral tradition concerned with correct behavior, with the fact that knowledge is a proportion between what you are and what you know."[6] Clemente's role as a student was a passive one, as he later recalled: "At the time, I was very surprised by the whole situation that was going on there between this man and his four students. I didn't really know what to think of it, but I was extremely impressed, watching these things."[7]

During this first visit Clemente kept a notebook and made numerous small India ink drawings (p. 61). These sketches mark the beginning of a vast body of ideogrammatic images, symbols, and emblems that Clemente would accumulate throughout the 1970s, and that would serve as a repositorium of imagery for his work throughout the 1980s. The drawings represent a pure play of ideas, and were created and assembled without any concern for order or arrangement. They were, quite simply, an aggregation of visual elements persistent enough to force themselves onto paper. As a condensed, informal record of his visual thinking during these crucial years, these drawings underscore the notational (as opposed to representational) aspect of Clemente's art.

When Clemente returned to Rome after his first trip to India, the letdown he felt was enormous. "To come back and look at the dullness . . . the eyes were so lifeless,"[8] he recalled wistfully. Clemente resumed life in Rome, working now to integrate into his life and work the radically altered view that India had offered. The sheer diversity of life in India proved to be the most lasting impression that Clemente carried away following this visit. While the experience opened up an enormous range of expressive possibilities he had not known in Rome, it also introduced a set of perplexities that would consume him for the next decade. The cultural multiformity of India led Clemente to accept fragmentation and stylistic diversity in art, in contradistinction to the prevailing cultural hegemony of the West. By abandoning the traditional hierarchical ordering of experience, Clemente was seeking a more open form that was able to accommodate the influx of new factors brought to the fore in India: eros, the psychic imagination, the mutability of meaning, and the discontinuity of experience: "My overall strategy or view as an artist is to accept fragmentation, and to see what comes of it—if anything. . . . Technically, this means I do not arrange the mediums and images I work with in any hierarchy of value. One is as good as another for me. All the images have the same expressive weight, and I have no preferred medium. . . . I believe in the dignity of each of the different levels and parts of the self. I don't want to lose any of them. To me they each exist simultaneously, not hierarchically. . . . One is not better than another. I do not prefer one over another. So that to lose one is in a sense to lose all."[9] To attempt to reduce a work, idea, or emotion to its constituent parts and assign each a value is an impossibility, all the more so with respect to art. There is no correct order because there is no correct interpretation. The elements that constitute a work of art are wedded to their form, which is in turn wedded to the physical fact of its making. It is a complex, a whole made up of interrelated parts, each of which is a fundamental determinant in the meaning of the work.

In 1974 Clemente again headed East. For nearly a year he traveled throughout Afghanistan with his friend and fellow artist Alighiero Boetti, with an extended stay in Kabul, where Boetti operated a hostel and café. Boetti, who is twelve years Clemente's senior, was well established as a leading figure in the Arte Povera movement. At the time, the wide range of ideas and influences that Boetti utilized in his art had great appeal for Clemente: "The iconography of his work was very eclectic," he later recalled. "It really took from a lot of different things. The ideas behind it derived in large part from the French—Lacanian ideas of eccentricity, autonomy, criticism of politics. But the focus, the soul of this whole system, was that you had to build your own territory. You have to build your own territory just for the fact that it has to have a reality of its own, that it exists apart from everything else."[10] Like Clemente, Boetti had left Rome in disgust with the narrowness of the art world and the strangle hold on aesthetic discourse held by critics and intellectuals. While in Afghanistan, Boetti employed local embroiderers to create a series of canvases using ambiguous and poetical word plays (see Figure 1). The trip was, in a sense, an unofficial apprenticeship for Clemente. Upon his return in 1975, Rome seemed even more confining, and the following year he left for India for a second time, with his future wife Alba.

The three months Clemente spent in India in 1976 were divided among Delhi, Benares, and Madras. For a month in Delhi he and Alba slept along the banks of the Ganges in an encampment of Tibetan monks. There he kept a notebook that he later used as a collaged element in the portfolio *Early Morning Exercises,* to accompany poems by the Boston writer John Wieners (p. 182). From Delhi they traveled to Benares, the seat of classical learning in India. Again, they lived along the banks of the Ganges, visiting temples and participating in the religious life of the holy city. After several weeks in Benares, the Clementes traveled to Madras, lured by the many temples and sacred cities of the Dravidian south.

Throughout the 1970s the tendency toward inclusiveness in Clemente's work is everywhere evident. If the overriding minimalist concern of the time was how much of the outside world could be *excluded* from art, Clemente's concern soon became how much of the outside world could be *included.* In his Italian years we see Clemente involved in the fundamental struggle to create a structure or form able to accommodate the tremendous variety of ideas and styles that possessed him. Ultimately, however, the borrowings would not do. But it was not until his third India visit, in 1977, that Clemente discovered this form, which turned out to be a kind of formlessness.

The adaptation of outside systems to art was a shared preoccupation among many artists of the late 1960s and early 1970s. As part of their art-making activities, artists were pursuing systems of thought and ways of organizing information as diverse as archaeology, mathematics, semiotics, and philosophical discourse. It would be a mistake to situate Clemente in opposition to such artists, since he clearly absorbed so much of their work. Yet inevitably he rejected such approaches, most frequently citing what he felt to be the poverty of the appearance of the works of art themselves, and especially their failure to embody the richness of the process behind their creation. Among such artists only Joseph Beuys remained an exemplary figure for him, in large part, as Clemente explained, through his ritualistic approach to art and his shamanistic willingness to regard himself as the instrument upon which the forces of inspiration played (see Figure 7).

Conceptualism, earthworks, video and performance art—so much of the art of the late 1960s and early 1970s was about expanding the formal vocabulary of art by utilizing other media and methods. The task Clemente was engaged in was not to expand the formal vocabulary; he was in fact seeking a return to traditional media and working methods. He was instead searching for a means to reanimate art with the philosophical, religious, and hermetic import that had existed in centuries past. He was looking forward with one eye and backward with the other. His contemporaries' loss of faith in painting as a viable expression was undeniable; the tremendous weight of the tradition alone seemed reason enough to abandon it. But for Clemente, who was schooled in the classics, this was precisely the allure: to engage the tradition, and to treat its historical canon of images and styles as one more element with which to work.

During this period, Clemente's travels in India confirmed his need to reinvest art with a sense of pleasure and fantasy, and to search out its roots in the psychic imagination. India brought about in him a reawakening of interest in the ritualistic origins of art, not the least of which was the reaffirmation of sexuality (regarded by Tantrists as an intrinsically divine quality). Eros, once a prime motivator in Western art, has never lost its power in Indian art. It is rare in our day that a work of art can still shock, but Clemente's blatant expositions of sexuality regularly elicit strong reactions from viewing audiences. By aiming directly at society's taboos and exposing them, Clemente calls attention to our collective sexual anxieties. Yet the artist's intention is not to shock but to explore the erotic impulse impassively—to deny the possibility that one might be intimidated by one's own desires. From the Hindu standpoint, the correct attitude would be one of acceptance, followed by detachment.

During Clemente's return to India in 1977, he felt an even greater sense of despair toward his homeland than he did in 1973. Enormous disillusion and considerable persecution followed the rebellions of 1968, polarizing Italian society along political lines and splintering radical groups previously united. On a personal level, Clemente had reached a period of transition in his work, having fully rejected the narrow academicism of the Italian art scene, while still not knowing how to deal with the rush of ideas and images that flowed ceaselessly out of his life and experience. "In 1977 the degree of fermentation and bankruptcy of all the ideas and all the people I knew was so high . . . that I didn't really feel bound to anything anymore."[11] To this dilemma, India was to prove the way out.

The overwhelming variety of subjects and styles, visions and emotions, and techniques and materials that coexisted in Indian life and art helped Clemente to free himself from the narrow world of the Italian avant-garde. Yet ultimately his response to the energy and vitality of Indian art had not so much to do with a reaction against the austerity of Western minimalism and conceptualism as it did with the simple fact that Indian notions of aesthetics were more closely allied with his own. The cultural multiformity of India appealed to his natural eclecticism and freed him to pursue the stylistic diversity he had been seeking. The many years of dissolution Clemente experienced in Italy proved a direct pathway to his realization of the Hindu tenet that the breaking up or destruction of a thing is a necessary part of its renewal. For him, after having torn down all previous ideas and conventions he had been working with, India became the place of regeneration. "My work really came together in 1977 on this trip," he later recalled.[12]

Between February and May of 1977 the Clementes returned to Madras, dividing their time between the Connemara Hotel and the Theosophical Society. The profusion of drawings, watercolors, and pastels continued unabated, and many of these were included in a handmade catalogue, *Undae clemente flamina pulsae*, printed in Madras and issued the following year for an exhibition at Art & Project in Amsterdam (see Figure 16). The hesitant, tenuous quality that characterized many of Clemente's Indian drawings of the previous year was here replaced by a more forceful and openly playful quality; we see him now engaging the actuality of India. Also evident is a growing fascination with Indian popular culture, which would prove a constant source of inspiration in future years.

Clemente's love for the popular arts of India is part of a larger attraction to the notion of degenerated forms of the classical deistic tradition, both East and West. For any artist born and raised in Italy, the burden of a classical tradition stretching from antiquity to the Renaissance to the present is something one can seemingly neither afford to ignore nor risk to engage. If the tradition assumes museum status, then the artist is relegated to the position of curator and must be content with footnoting the past. Yet to engage such an immense cultural catalogue directly can prove equally oppressive. Thus for the artist it is a matter of constantly finding new use for outdated currency, and here the key is adaptability, of which Indians are masters. One must negotiate a thin line between the living and the dead, as Aldous Huxley once noted: "It isn't a matter of forgetting. What one has to learn is how to remember and yet be free of the past. How to be there with the dead and yet still be here, on the spot, with the living."[13] While this dilemma resulted in a kind of historical schizo-

Figure 17. Page from a Hindu comic book
India, c. 1980
Collection of Francesco and Alba Clemente, New York

Figure 18. Cover of a Hindu comic book
India, c. 1980
Collection of Francesco and Alba Clemente, New York

Figure 19. Campaign poster for the former film star
M. G. Ramachandran and the Two Leaf political party,
Tamil Nadu, India, c. 1985

phrenia or alienation in much of the West, Clemente found that the artisans he encountered in India shared a far more integrated relationship with their past, due in large part to the custom of handing down ideas and skills from one generation to the next. In this respect the Indian tradition of oral transmission of knowledge exists in contradistinction to the Western impulse to objectify knowledge, reducing it to the level of technique or materiality, and divorcing it from the function from which it derives.

While the rich historical traditions of classical Indian art provided a deep well of inspiration to Clemente, it was the popular arts of India that captured his painter's sense of fancy. These innumerable, common manifestations of Indian culture exist everywhere—advertising, movie placards, painted plaster statuettes of Hindu deities, postcards and souvenir books sold at temples and shrines, greeting cards depicting stars of soap operas or B-movies, comic books that retell the great epics or the lives of holy men—the list is endless (see Figures 17–19). Excessively vivid, cheap, and gaudy in appearance and quality, these contemporary artifacts have always held an extraordinary allure for Clemente. Inevitably, within a few days of his arrival in Madras, his studio is filled with such objects, which often function as a kind of mental backdrop for his work, in much the same way that the drone exists as a background constant in Indian music. These pop relics possess the same rhythmic design and purity of color as the fine arts from which they derive, but their creators are unconcerned with aesthetic considerations or theory. Rather these manifestations comprise a genuine urban folk art in a modernistic context: they are made by nonprofessionals and directed at the emotions. Full of luster and ornament, they are in many ways closer to what the classical arts of the frieze, fresco, or miniature would have looked like when first created. If art, as has been often said, is a way of imbuing the commonplace with a feeling of the sublime, then these popular creations might be said to be a way of treating the sublime with a sense of the commonplace. They represent not so much a deflation of the masterpiece, but a popular aspiration toward such an ideal. Responding to their honesty, energy, and veracity, Clemente is unwilling to accept the idea that the impulses behind classical Indian art—joy, sensuality, extravagance—are limited to past creations.

The Clementes returned to Italy in 1977 for the birth of their first daughter, Chiara, but eight months later, in the spring of 1978, they were again in India, visiting Kashmir and Pelgam in the Himalayas, and passing the summer in Delhi. In September they again journeyed to Madras, staying on for ten months, first at the Theosophical Society and later in a rented house in a garden compound on the grounds adjoining the Krishnamurti Foundation.

Madras is a city of three million people, sprawled across nine miles of gentle, winding seacoast on the Bay of Bengal. An ample harbor makes it a port of call for sea freighters, and the two major railway lines of southern India share a vast, cavernous terminal there. It is a relatively recent city, founded in 1639 as an English trading post, and later briefly held by the Portuguese and French. Madras is the capital of India's southernmost state, Tamil Nadu, and is a chief commercial city known for its glass, cement, and iron works, its cotton mills, and acres of flower plantations for the thriving trade in perfumes and essential oils. The major spoken language is Tamil, an ancient classical tongue that has survived virtually unchanged for twenty-five hundred years. Its native inhabitants are Dravidians, a purely linguistic term that describes the many peoples who once extended their domain across the entire subcontinent.

If the physical charms of Madras are gentle, the climatic extremes are not. Temperatures regularly range between 100 and 120 degrees Fahrenheit from early spring to late summer, and violent monsoons lasting six to eight weeks inundate the city twice yearly. It is during the palpable boredom of these stretches of heat and rain that Clemente works best, on the floors or verandas of rented houses or hotel rooms, or in a tiny backroom studio he keeps at

Figure 20. C. T. Nachiappan and Francesco Clemente, Ramana Maharshi ashram, Tiruvannamalai, India, 1984

Figure 21. Postcard of Hanuman, the Hindu monkey god, Madras, 1985

Figure 22. Francesco Clemente
Hanuman Books logo, 1986
Ink on paper, 4 x 3″ (10.2 x 7.6 cm)
Collection of Francesco and Alba Clemente,
New York

the Kalakshetra Press, a letterpress printing house presided over by his close friend C. T. Nachiappan (see Figures 20–24).[14] Both the quality and quantity of his art often seem to be inextricably equated with the degree of physical discomfort that must be endured during its creation.

Clemente's reasons for settling in Madras were largely due to the fact that it was a city where space, supplies, labor, and shipping could all be secured with a reasonable amount of perseverance. His reasons for staying were its proximity to several dozen temples and holy sites scattered across the state of Tamil Nadu; its wealth of classical musicians and dancers and the yearly Carnatic music festival; and its long tradition of philosophical learning centered around the Theosophical Society and the neighboring Krishnamurti Foundation.

Founded in New York City in 1875 by Helena P. Blavatsky and Henry S. Olcott, Theosophists organize themselves under the motto "All Religions Are One."[15] Theosophy was an eclectic movement, drawing influence from prevailing schools of occultism of the time — mesmerism, Swedenborgianism, Freemasonry, and Rosicrucianism — with heavy borrowings from the newly rediscovered religions of Egypt and India. From its inception Theosophy was also a pioneering social force, with its members advocating fair treatment for the American Indians, equal rights for women, prison reform, higher wages for workers, the right of labor to organize, and a host of other liberal causes. Under the leadership of the Englishwoman Annie Besant, the Theosophical Society in Madras became a focal point of the Indian National Congress and the movement for independence from Britain, earning it a position of great affection in the hearts of the citizens of Madras.

The religious eclecticism of the Theosophists and their antipathy to the Catholic Church held great appeal for William Butler Yeats, George William Russell (Æ), MacGregor Mathers, and many other members of the Irish literary renaissance in the early 1900s. The professed desire of the Theosophists to merge science, art, and religion, and their hostility to the rampant materialism of the industrial age attracted such international artist-members as Piet Mondrian, Max Beckmann, Arnold Schoenberg, Marsden Hartley, and Wassily Kandinsky, with the latter attributing his theories of abstract painting in part to Theosophical notions. With a sizable endowment, an ample library, and the genteel inhabitants of its residence hall, the Theosophical Society in Madras maintains itself as a center for the pursuit of occult and esoteric knowledge. It provides an anachronistic setting, a retreat from the world into simpler times, when the hopes for a world religion were still an ideal to be striven for. As Clemente later recounted:

> The Theosophical Society is like a modern painting in a modern museum, you know. Being there is like being in the waters in which people like Mondrian were fishing. There is again this hope of finding a universal language of human experience which everyone could use all over the earth. The result of the Theosophical Society has been the thought of Krishnamurti, who resembles the American Expressionist painters in the sense that he said one must give up all these symbols, that they all belong to talk, and talk is bound by time, and freedom and unity are not within the boundaries of time. The Society is a place where you can still breathe the spirit of the 20's and the hopes of the 20's — and at the same time you can understand that spirit gave rise to something like American Expressionism, people like Clyfford Still or Franz Kline.[16]

Clemente's remarks regarding the pleasantly anachronistic ideals of the Theosophical Society are of interest for the connection he draws between the philosophy of Krishnamurti and the notions of the sublime as expressed by many of the American Abstract Expressionist painters.[17] A statement summarizing the credo of his contemporaries, chosen from the writings of Barnett Newman, could have easily been spoken by Krishnamurti himself: "We are freeing ourselves of the impediments of memory, association, nostalgia, legend, myth, or

Figure 23. Cover of *Sayings of the Holy Mother* (Madras: Weldun Press, 1983). Books such as these were the prototypes for the Hanuman Books, published by Francesco Clemente and Raymond Foye, and printed by C. T. Nachiappan

Figure 24. Cover of Eileen Myles, *Bread and Water* (Madras and New York: Hanuman Books, 1987)

Figure 25. Jiddu Krishnamurti, Theosophical Society, Madras, c. 1915

what have you, that have been the devices of Western European painting. Instead of making *cathedrals* out of Christ, man, or 'life,' we are making it out of ourselves, out of our own feelings. The image we produce is the self-evident one of revelation, real and concrete, that can be understood by anyone who will look at it without the nostalgic glasses of history."[18]

Jiddu Krishnamurti (his first name was later dropped) was discovered swimming off the beach in Madras in 1909 by C. W. Leadbeater, second in command at the Theosophical Society at Adayar, a district of Madras (Figure 25). Recognizing an extraordinary aura surrounding the fourteen-year-old boy, Leadbeater came to believe that this was the World Teacher, or Bodhisattva, whose coming both Blavatsky and Besant had predicted. Krishnamurti was soon placed under the guardianship of the Theosophical Society for a ten-year period of education and spiritual training in India and England. Eventually failing his entrance examinations at Oxford, he stayed on in London and developed a fondness for the theater, Saville Row tailors, and British motor cars. He returned to Madras in 1921 to head a special order of the Society that had been created for him. In 1929, with his followers numbering well over ten thousand, Krishnamurti renounced his title of World Teacher. Speaking in the presence of Mrs. Besant and three thousand believers, he denounced his disciples as "false, hypocritical people following me," and the Theosophical Society as an "absurd . . . structure."[19] He condemned all religions, sects, and authority, and insisted upon the solitary path of the individual seeking enlightenment. Turning from the religious to the secular, Krishnamurti began a fifty-five-year journey as teacher and philosopher. While his thought embodied the essence of Buddhist, Hindu, and Western religious teachings, he insisted upon dispensing with the ritual trappings that these beliefs promote. (He once told Aldous Huxley that meditating on objects such as lotuses, lights, gods, and goddesses might lead to insanity.) Instead, Krishnamurti's meditations focused unrelentingly on the nature of time, perception, and awareness *in the present moment,* while his notion of beauty closely paralleled the Western concept of the sublime.

Although Clemente has noted that he "never got around" to attending a single meeting at the Theosophical Society in Madras (eventually prompting looks of gentle consternation from some members), he often made use of their vast library, and always enjoyed the company of other residents and visiting guests.[20] The Clementes occupied a large, single room on the third floor of the Leadbeater Chambers, a stately English colonial-style residence hall (Figure 26). Their austere room contained a bed with white mosquito netting, writing desk, chair, and ceiling fan, opening onto a huge veranda overlooking the Bay of Bengal. Clemente would spend hours on this veranda, practicing yoga, reading the teachings of Krishnamurti and Ramana Maharshi, and creating the eighty-five drawings that came to be known as "The Pondicherry Pastels" (pp. 65–68).

"The Pondicherry Pastels" take their name from the former French colonial port, just south of Madras, along the east coast of India. Although some of the works were created there, the majority were made in Madras. (The title was attached because some of the pastels were drawn on handmade paper from the Sri Aurobindo ashram in Auroville, just outside of Pondicherry [see Figure 27].) They are among Clemente's most unique and memorable works, due in part to their intimate scale and the innocent, artless clarity with which they are drawn. With obvious delight and in a typically involute manner, in this series Clemente delves into the many conventions governing depiction. The pastels are influenced by both classical Indian miniatures and contemporary popular imagery. Clemente explores the iconographic import of common objects (Figure 28), portraits, animals, and fauna in rich colors evocative of the subcontinent. The notion of the commonplace in both subject and materials is a central theme in the series, and one that the artist would return to throughout the next decade. In discussing a group of pastels created a decade later (and with striking thematic similarities), Clemente recalled his concerns of that time: "For me this series was a return to a certain language that I was fascinated with fantasizing about in my early work: about

Figure 26. Clemente on the veranda of the Leadbeater Chambers, Theosophical Society, Madras, 1979

Figure 27. Clemente dyeing handmade paper with local craftsmen, Madras, 1983

Figure 28. Francesco Clemente
Plate from *Happier Than Piero*, 1979
Pastel on paper, 6⅜ x 3⁹⁄₁₆″ (16.2 x 9 cm)
Anthony d'Offay Gallery, London

clichés and commonplaces, assuming that a commonplace is taken literally as "a place in common" among people in a time when there is nothing in common among anybody. A place where many different meanings of people connect."[21]

This notion of the common is a persistent desire, a *longing,* that runs like a subtext through Clemente's work. While he is often thought of as an artist devoted to the arcane or occult aspects of culture, there is an equally persistent strain to his work that insists upon the elemental: that which is integral or essential to mankind and shared by all regardless of place, privilege, or social status. Indeed, it is the subtle play between the opposing impulses of familiarity and concealment that lends his work its special tension.

"The Pondicherry Pastels" represent an intermediate zone between the austerity of Clemente's Roman works and the extravagance of his so-called Neo-Expressionist period. It is significant that it was these works that Clemente chose to show at his first solo exhibition in New York City in 1980. It is difficult today to recapture that odd admixture of feelings one had as a viewer, confronted for the first time by these seemingly modest works, and being genuinely displaced by their *otherness,* both geographical and aesthetic. They did not refer to any other art, nor were they a reaction to such: they simply represented one of those rare achievements in art—a new place in which to exist.

"The Pondicherry Pastels" are also significant in that they firmly establish a method that Clemente would settle into throughout his mature career—that of working in series. Clemente has always been interested in what one might call organizing principles: how and why objects or ideas are grouped according to subject, size, shape, number, or that most arbitrary of all methods, alphabetization, and in what ways these structures impart meaning to their individual elements. While much of his work is about fragmentation, there exists a larger theme of interdependence. The organization of disparate elements, whether governed by natural or imaginary laws, is a constant source of fascination for Clemente: the plant kingdom as ordered by Linnaeus, the heavens as charted by John Dee, or the human body as schematized by the Tantrists (see Figure 29). Such arrangements aspire to the divine pattern that recurs in the fragmentary images of the fallen world, fulfilled in the symbolic realm where ultimately everything symbolizes everything else. Working in series also opens up a sort of analogical chain reaction where image begets image and meaning generates meaning. The "theme and variation" aspect of serial work likewise allows the artist to explore the same idea in different contexts until the circuit is closed or the idea exhausted.

In the 1980s Clemente established a pattern of making extended biyearly visits to India. Paradoxically, the country was by now becoming both increasingly familiar *and* exotic. For Clemente, India came to serve as a much-needed clearing, both physical and psychic, as well as a traveling back through time to an Ur culture, where the gods of Hinduism echo the chthonic origins of Greek religion. It was this quality of resonance, of one culture resounding within another, that took on increasing importance in his art.

The opportunity to work with craftspeople of all sorts has always been an important part of Clemente's working methodology. This is particularly so in India, where he regularly employs the skills of the young miniature painters of Jaipur and Orissa, the papermakers of Pondicherry, and the Tamil billboard painters who are responsible for the remarkable movie placards that adorn the major thoroughfares of Madras. In each case, Clemente is seeking to participate in the sensibility of another, in a kind of literal realization of Arthur Rimbaud's remark that "I is an Other."[22] By allowing his creativity to flow through another person, Clemente likewise gains a desired conceptual distance from himself and his work. It is a method of circumventing the habit of one's own impulses, and a way of introducing an element of chance or misunderstanding into the work, which has always appealed to Clemente's highly developed sense of ambivalence.

Figure 29. Francesco Clemente
Untitled, 1985
Oil on aluminum, mounted on honeycomb fiberglass;
67 x 41″ (170.2 x 104.1 cm)
Private Collection, Courtesy Sperone Westwater,
New York

Figure 30. Francesco Clemente
Untitled, 1985
Pastel on paper, 12³/₁₆ x 12³/₁₆″ (31 x 31 cm)
Courtesy Sperone Westwater, New York

The subject of collaboration has often been problematical for viewers and critics of Clemente's work, for nothing is so antithetical or unsettling to our Western notion of the artist-as-hero than this willful relinquishing of control. But what is gained are the resources, knowledge, and skill that the craftspeople bring to bear upon the work, based upon their understanding of a centuries-old tradition. Clemente's pleasure in engaging such a tradition—and in casting it in contemporary terms with a total absence of sentimentality—has proven a continual source of delight in his work. When an artist effectively engages a tradition, as Ezra Pound noted, he not only partakes in the spirit of past knowledge, but also updates that tradition and lends it momentum. Thus time and again in Clemente's work we see this fascination with tradition and with new uses for archaic currency. Indians are masters of adaptability, and in India it often seems there is virtually no custom or idea from earlier times that does not have its present-day usage. For Clemente, it is the shape of the idea that matters—the form itself. The specific contents, whether words or images, are, throughout the ages, interchangeable. It is the forms alone that endure.

It was during his 1985 stay in Madras that Clemente created some of the most ambitious works on paper of his career, in a series that plays upon the theme of unity and duality. *The Four Corners* (p. 79) is a vast gouache on sheets of handmade Pondicherry paper, joined together with strips of cotton muslin. The image was executed with the assistance of Tamil sign painters, whose flat, bold style, complemented by gentle shadings, greatly appealed to Clemente. A vast hand rises from the sea against a starry sky, while man's fate, the "map" of the hand, is superimposed with a map of the world. In selecting the hand as subject for this and related gouaches (see Figure 34 and p. 63), Clemente has chosen the universal archetypal image that has served man from prehistoric times to the present. It is the image of man's destiny: the palm as a signpost to personal fate—or simply to the inevitable future. That the artist has enlarged the hand to such gigantic proportions induces a sense of awe, a sense of the dreadful power that is among the first intimations of religions both Eastern and Western: the need to stay on the right side of the Prime Mover.

The image of the hand occurs throughout Clemente's work (see Figure 30 and pp. 176–77); along with the face it is the most versatile and visible part of the body, and a source of near limitless expression. Anthropologists have often speculated that visual communication preceded verbal communication in the history of mankind. An elaborate system of hand gestures was developed, and it is from these that our written alphabet derives. In many ancient religions these gestures survive as ritual invocations. The traditional rabbinical blessing in Orthodox Judaism is performed by a member of the hereditary priestly caste with the fingers of one hand, and with the congregation's eyes scrupulously averted. Many gods of the Buddhist and Hindu pantheon are endowed with numerous hands, and in Hinduism each part of a devotee's hand is sacred, belonging to a god or goddess. A vast array of delicate, static hand poses are used in the Bharata Natyam, the classical dance of southern India, which Clemente so deeply admires. These poses are in turn derived from mudras, the ritual hand poses of the Buddhist and Hindu priests. Mudras are sacred gestures, symbolic of mantras, that are used in evoking deities or channeling cosmic powers. In this light, Clemente's Madras gouaches can be seen as contemporary mudras—visual formulas meant to evoke the elemental themes common to all religions, the wonder and awe of creation.

The companion works to the "hand" gouaches from 1985 include *Day and Night* (Figure 31), *Hermaphrodite, Boy, Girl,* and *Untitled* (Figure 32). If the "hand" gouaches can be said to depict unity, their counterparts can be said to represent binary divisions—day and night, male and female, silence and speech, physics and metaphysics, body and mind, north and south, east and west—each revolving around the other in mutual dependency. The figures are surrounded by the Theosophist's "etheric" envelope, where thoughts and impulses

Figure 31. Francesco Clemente
Day and Night, 1985
Gouache on handmade paper, 94 x 130″ (238.8 x 330.2 cm)
Private Collection

Figure 32. Francesco Clemente
Untitled, 1985
Gouache on handmade paper, 94 x 130″ (238.8 x 330.2 cm)
Private Collection, Courtesy Sperone Westwater,
New York

become, for a time, living creatures. If unity belongs to the gods, disunity is man's lot. "Oneself is like half a fragment," said the sage Yajnavalkya.[23] In each of these gouaches a figure is torn between the two aspects of his nature in a world of tugging opposites. By giving in to these illusions, seeking the gratification of his desires, man further descends into the torpor of his existence. To experience the unity of the divine realm is the ultimate goal in the practice of yoga, but as in Antonin Artaud's observation, which Clemente is fond of quoting, the four-thousand-year-old system of yoga is easily dissolved by the reality of a simple toothache.[24]

In time, India became the ideal working environment for Clemente, and the works he has created there are possessed with an animated glow quite unlike those made in Rome or New York. Looking back over the decade and a half that Clemente has worked and dwelled in India, one is struck by not merely the diversity of subjects, styles, and techniques that he has engaged, but also by the equally various states of mind that he has explored in his work. The true subject of Clemente's art is consciousness itself, and in this respect his works on paper comprise a graph of the mind in many forms—history, myth, imaginings, musings, poetry, symbols, meditations, notations, inscriptions, ideographs, hieroglyphs—each forming a fragment of a greater whole, which might be termed a belief. For Clemente drawing is not an afterthought or embellishment or appendage to painting but rather the seed of it. The drawings are actual road maps of the ideas contained within the paintings. The primacy of drawing in Clemente's work lies in the fact that it is not only the technical foundation of his art but the conceptual basis as well. The extraordinary body of drawings that Clemente produced between 1970 and 1980 (some of which precede the paintings by ten years) are the record of a personal struggle to fix an image, to give permanent form to a set of vastly shifting emotional states. In this attempt to find some equivalence, the coherence of the work is not reliant upon any external logic or system, but rather upon the nature and process of the artist's intuition, intellect, and temperament. The viewer is not in a position to explain or even to "understand," but simply to behold.

1. Donald Kuspit, "Clemente Explores Clemente," *Contemporanea*, vol. 2, no. 7 (October 1989), p. 40.

2. *Kena Upanishads*, II, 3; quoted in *Francesco Clemente: India* (Pasadena, 1986), n.p.

3. Interview with Rainer Crone and Georgia Marsh, May 1986; this quote is taken from the unedited transcripts that were later published in Crone and Marsh, *Francesco Clemente: An Interview with Francesco Clemente* (New York, 1987).

4. Crone and Marsh, *Clemente,* p. 18. A book-length series of interviews conducted at the artist's studio in New York in May of 1986, this is by far the best introduction to the artist's work in his own words.

5. Kuspit, "Clemente," p. 39.

6. Crone and Marsh, *Clemente,* p. 19.

7. Ibid., p. 22.

8. Ibid., p. 24.

9. Kuspit, "Clemente," p. 40.

10. Crone and Marsh, unpublished transcripts.

11. Crone and Marsh, *Clemente,* p. 26.

12. Crone and Marsh, unpublished transcripts.

13. Aldous Huxley, *The Devils of Loudun,* quoted in B. S. Gupta, *The Glassy Essence: A Study of E. M. Forster, L. H. Myers, and Aldous Huxley in Relation to Indian Thought* (Kurukshetra, India, 1976), p. 239.

14. Nachiappan, printer, book designer, scholar, and devout Hindu, is the owner and publisher of the press. His jovial nature and vast knowledge of Indian art, religion, philosophy, and literature has made him a close friend and traveling companion to the Clemente family when residing in South India. Nachiappan is the printer of Hanuman Books, a series of miniature volumes of poetry and prose published and edited by Clemente and Raymond Foye. Based in format on Hindu prayer books widely available in India, Hanuman Books measure 3 x 4 inches. Named after the Hindu monkey god Hanuman, the press is devoted to publishing the works of poets, writers, artists, and philosophers whose works are valued by Clemente and Foye (see Figures 21–24). The series at present contains 42 titles. The complete list of authors includes John Wieners, David Trinidad, Eileen Myles, Taylor Mead, Francis Picabia, Henri Michaux, Amy Gerstler, John Ashbery, Herbert Huncke, Manuel Rosenthal, René Daumal, Bob Flanagan, Willem de Kooning, Cookie Mueller, Sandro Penna, Vincent Katz, Alain Daniélou, Edwin Denby, Max Beckmann, Gary Indiana, Jean Genet, Allen Ginsberg, René Guénon, Gregory Corso, Elaine Equi, Ronald Firbank, Rene Ricard, David Hockney, St. Teresa, Simone Weil, Jack Smith, Beauregard Houston-Montgomery, Bob Dylan, Richard Hell, Henry Geldzahler, Robert Creeley, Dodie Bellamy, and Jack Kerouac.

15. For an excellent history of Theosophy, see Bruce F. Campbell's *Ancient Wisdom Revived: A History of the Theosophical Movement* (Berkeley, 1980).

16. Crone and Marsh, unpublished transcripts.

17. The connection between Krishnamurti and the Abstract Expressionists can in fact be documented in the case of Jackson Pollock. Already conversant with the ideas of the Theosophists, Pollock spent the summer of 1929 at Krishnamurti's Star Camp in Ojai, California. Through his friend Frederick Schwankovsky, an intimate of Krishnamurti, Pollock entered the close circle of followers. In later life Pollock's widow, Lee Krasner, recalled him frequently mentioning the work of Krishnamurti. See Steven Naifeh and Gregory White Smith, *Jackson Pollock: An American Saga* (New York, 1989), pp. 129–31, 137–45, 151, 157, 821–22.

18. Barnett Newman, "The Sublime Is Now," *The Tiger's Eye* (December 1948), p. 53.

19. Pupul Jayakar, *Krishnamurti: A Biography* (San Francisco, 1986), pp. 77, 78.

20. Clemente in conversation with the author, 1985. Clemente was not a member of the Theosophical Society.

21. Francesco Clemente, interview with Lisa Phillips, March 27, 1989. The interview was conducted in English and all quotes are taken from this transcript. An edited version of the interview appeared in *Beaux Arts Magazine*, no. 69 (June 1989), pp. 91–95, 159–60, under the title "Exposition Clemente: Les Chemins de la sagesse," and included a summary in English.

22. Rimbaud to George Izambard, May 13, 1871; in Arthur Rimbaud, *Oeuvres completes* (Paris, 1972), p. 249.

23. Quoted in Philip Rawson, *Erotic Art of the East: The Sexual Theme in Oriental Painting and Sculpture* (New York, 1968), p. 31.

24. "Et le clou d'une douleur dentaire, le coup de marteau d'une chute accidentelle sur un os en disent plus sur les ténèbres de l'inconscient que toutes les recherches de la yoga." Antonin Artaud, "L'Homme et sa douleur," in Antonin Artaud, *Oeuvres completes*, vol. 14 (Paris, 1978), p. 205.

Untitled, 1973
Ink on paper
8¹⁄₂ x 5⁵⁄₁₆″ (21.6 x 13.5 cm)
Öffentliche Kunstsammlung,
Kupferstichkabinett, Basel. 1984.34

Untitled, 1973
Ink on paper
4⁵⁄₈ x 6¹⁄₈″ (11.8 x 15.6 cm)
Öffentliche Kunstsammlung,
Kupferstichkabinett, Basel. 1984.32

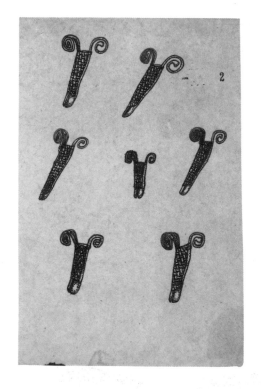

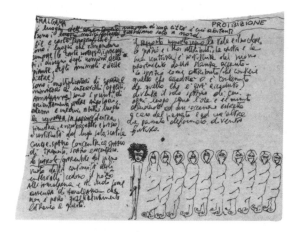

Untitled, 1974
Ink and pastel on graph paper
7¹⁄₈ x 5⁷⁄₈″ (18.1 x 15 cm)
Öffentliche Kunstsammlung,
Kupferstichkabinett, Basel. 1984.46

Untitled, 1974
Pencil on paper
9 x 5³⁄₈″ (22.9 x 13.7 cm)
Collection of Francesco and Alba Clemente,
New York

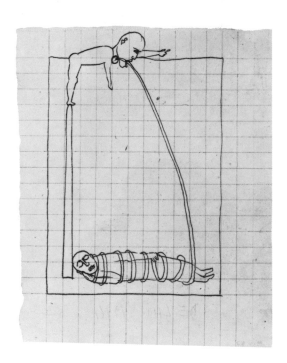

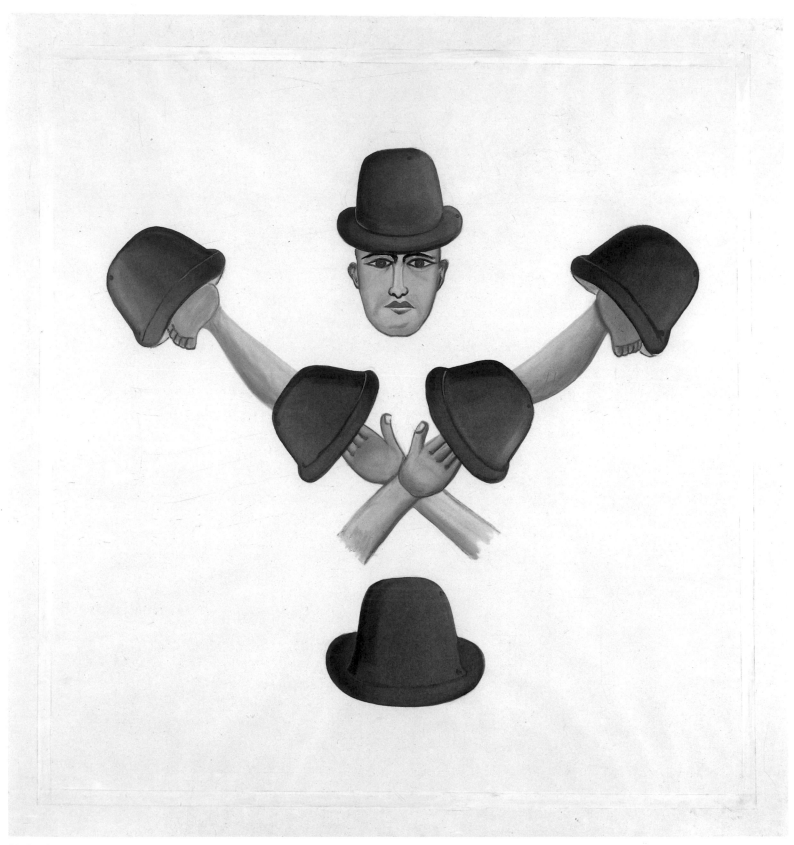

Under the Hat, 1978
Gouache on paper
60 x 57″ (152.4 x 144.8 cm)
IFIDA Health Care Group, Bryn Mawr,
Pennsylvania

Map of What Is Effortless, 1978
Gouache on paper
60 x 57" (152.4 x 144.8 cm)
Private Collection

Two Horizons, a Thousand, 1978
Gouache on paper
64 x 54½″ (162.6 x 138.3 cm)
Paul Maenz, Cologne

The Sick Rose, 1979
Nine pastels on paper
6³/₈ x 3¹/₂″ (16.2 x 9 cm) to 12⁵/₈ x 8″
(32 x 20.4 cm)
Anthony d'Offay Gallery, London

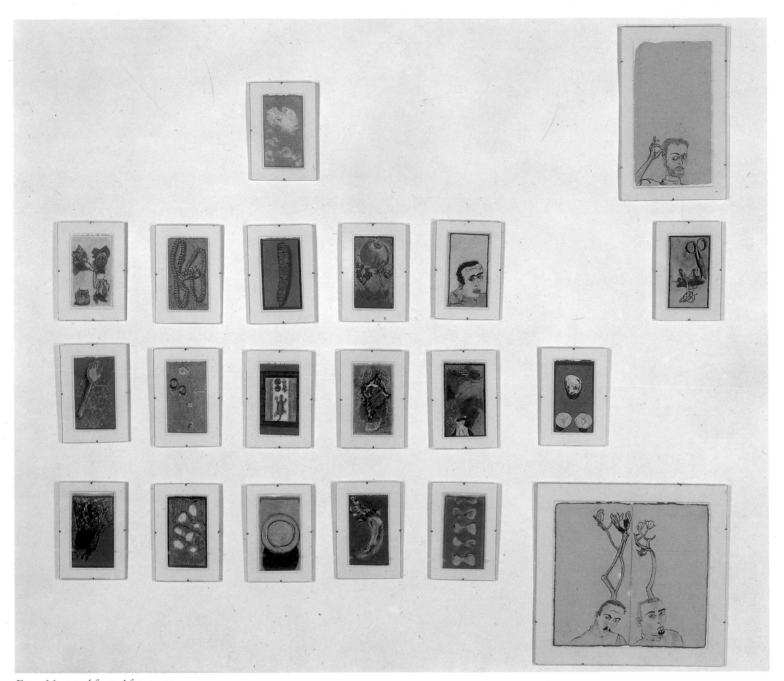

From Near and from Afar, 1979
Twenty pastels on paper
6³⁄₈ x 3¹⁄₂″ (16.2 x 9 cm) to 13 x 13³⁄₄″
(33 x 35 cm)
Anthony d'Offay Gallery, London

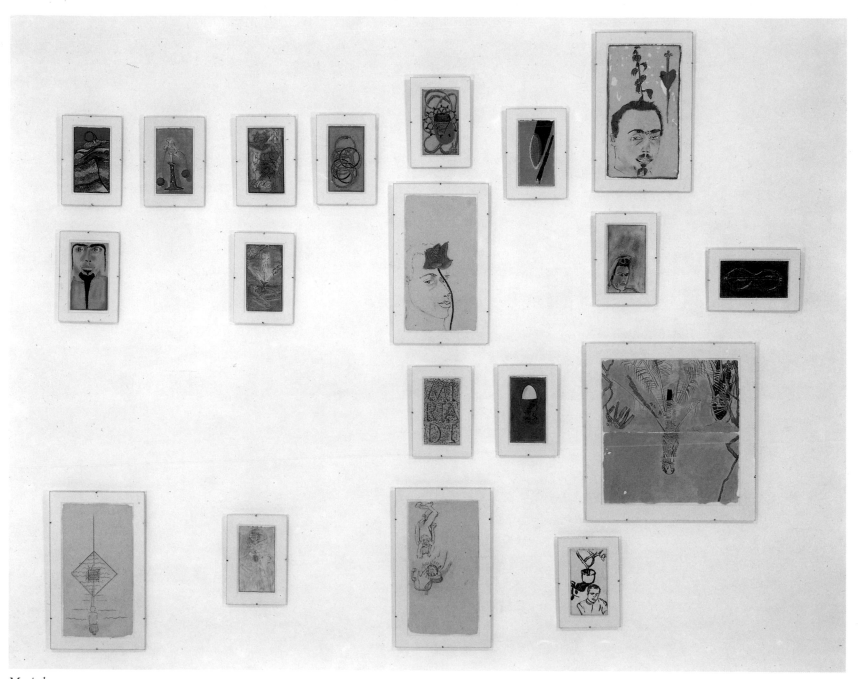

Myriads, 1979
Nineteen pastels on paper
6 3/8 x 3 1/2" (16.2 x 9 cm) to 13 3/4 x 13"
(35 x 33 cm)
Anthony d'Offay Gallery, London

Around and Very Close, 1979
Eleven pastels on paper
6 3/8 x 3 1/2″ (16.2 x 9 cm) and 6 7/8 x 13″
(17.5 x 33 cm)
Anthony d'Offay Gallery, London

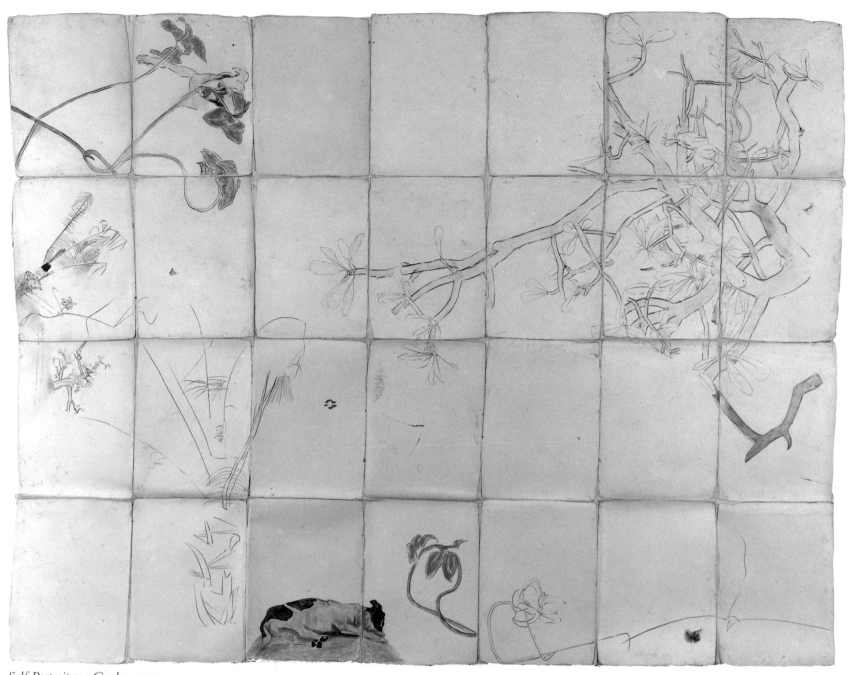

Self-Portrait as a Garden, 1979
Charcoal, gold paint, and dirt on twenty-eight
sheets of handmade paper, joined by cotton
strips
126 x 157½" (320 x 400 cm)
Private Collection, Courtesy Galerie Bruno
Bischofberger, Zurich

Sun, 1980
Gouache on twelve sheets of handmade
Pondicherry paper, joined by cotton strips
91 x 95″ (231.1 x 241.3 cm)
Philadelphia Museum of Art. Purchased:
Edward and Althea Budd Fund, Katharine
Levin Farrell Fund, and funds contributed by
Mrs. H. Gates Lloyd. 1984-118-1

Moon, 1980
Gouache on twelve sheets of handmade
Pondicherry paper, joined by cotton strips
96¾ x 91" (245.8 x 231.1 cm)
Collection of Alan Wanzenberg, New York

Hunger, 1980
Gouache on twelve sheets of handmade
Pondicherry paper, joined by cotton strips
96¹/₂ x 93¹/₂″ (245.1 x 237.5 cm)
Collection of Marion Stroud Swingle,
Elverson, Pennsylvania

Rain, 1980
Gouache on twelve sheets of handmade
Pondicherry paper, joined by cotton strips
94 x 95″ (238.8 x 241.3 cm)
Collection of Judy and Harvey Gushner,
Bryn Mawr, Pennsylvania

Interior Landscape, 1980
Pastel on paper
24 x 18″ (61 x 45.8 cm)
Courtesy Thomas Ammann, Zurich

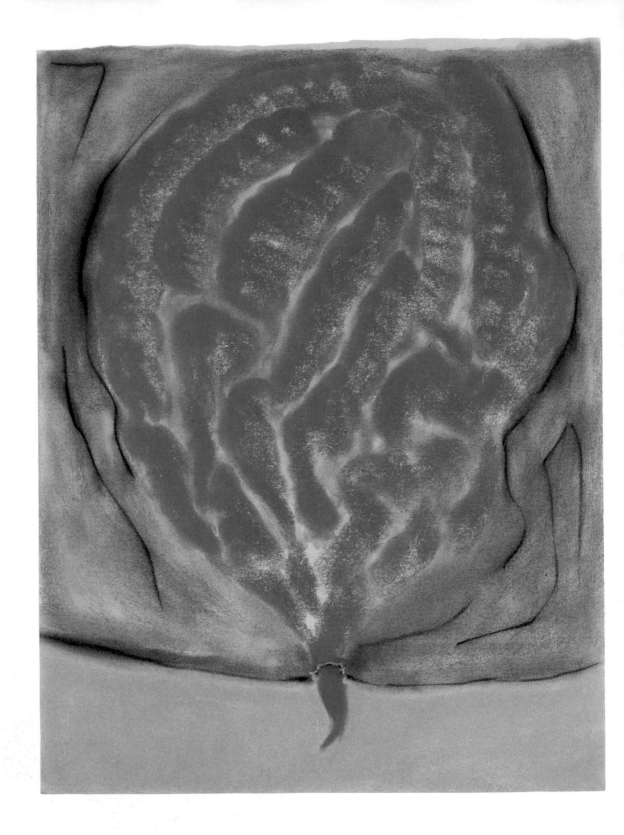

Caduceo, 1981
Pastel on paper
24 x 18″ (61 x 45.8 cm)
Collection of Joan S. Sonnabend, Boston

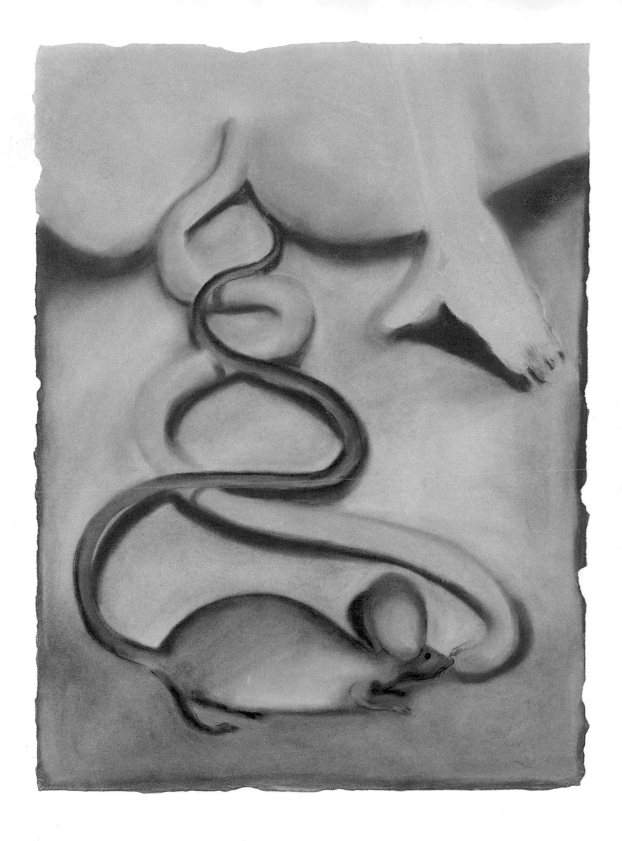

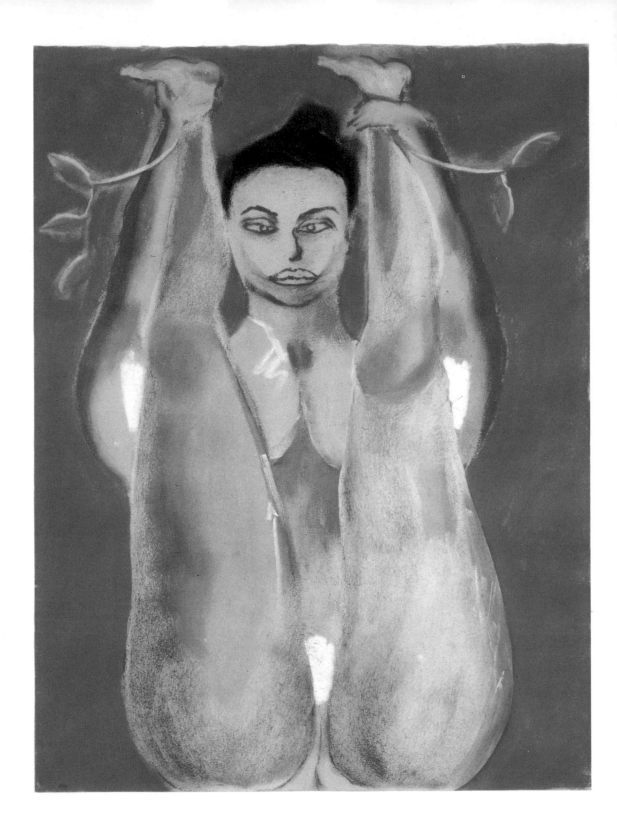

La mia ginnastica, 1982
Pastel on paper
24 x 18″ (61 x 45.8 cm)
Courtesy Thomas Ammann, Zurich

Inside, Outside, 1980
Gouache on nine sheets of handmade
Pondicherry paper, joined by cotton strips
67¾ x 92½" (172.1 x 235 cm)
Paul Maenz, Cologne

1152, 1983
Eleven papier-mâché sculptures
height of each 26¾″ (68 cm)
Collection of Francesco and Alba Clemente,
New York

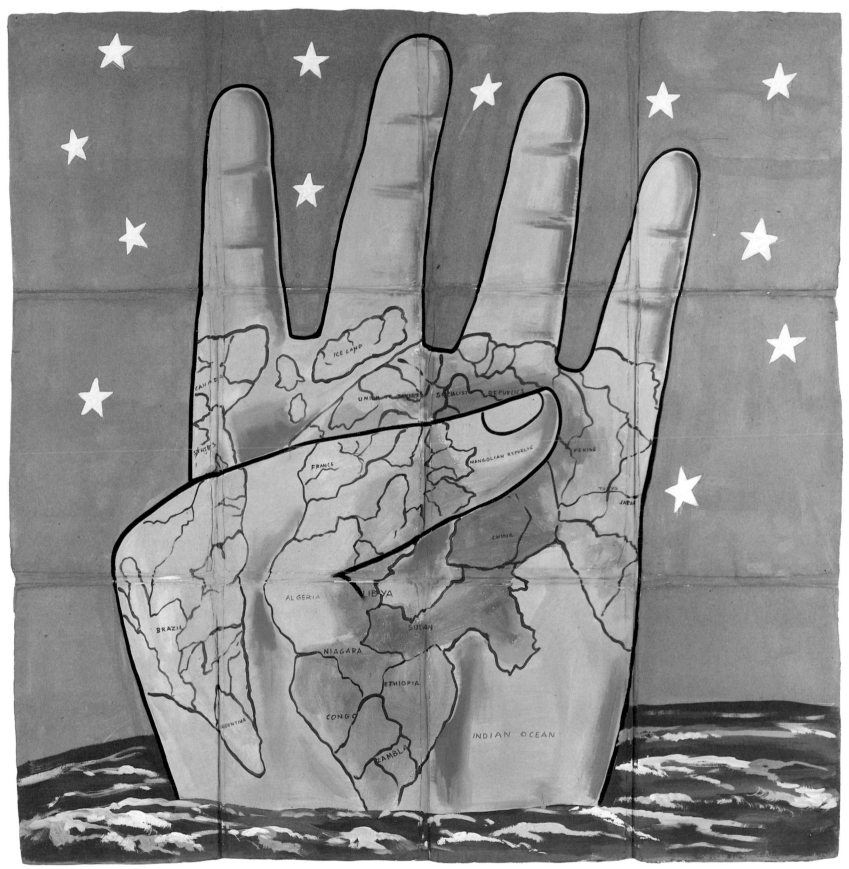

The Four Corners, 1985
Gouache on twelve sheets of handmade
Pondicherry paper, joined by cotton strips
94 x 94″ (238.8 x 238.8 cm)
Collection of Barbara Radice, Milan

No. XII from *CVIII*, 1985
Watercolor on handmade Pondicherry paper
10³/₄ x 8³/₁₆″ (27.4 x 20.8 cm)
Öffentliche Kunstsammlung,
Kupferstichkabinett, Basel

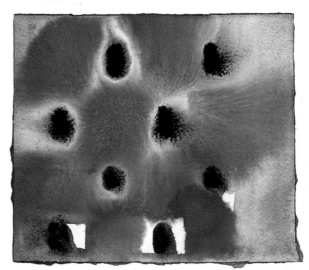

No. L from *CVIII*, 1985
Watercolor on handmade Pondicherry paper
8³/₄ x 10¹/₁₆″ (22.2 x 25.6 cm)
Öffentliche Kunstsammlung,
Kupferstichkabinett, Basel

No. XXXV from *CVIII*, 1985
Watercolor on handmade Pondicherry paper
7¹/₁₆ x 9¹¹/₁₆″ (17.9 x 24.6 cm)
Öffentliche Kunstsammlung,
Kupferstichkabinett, Basel

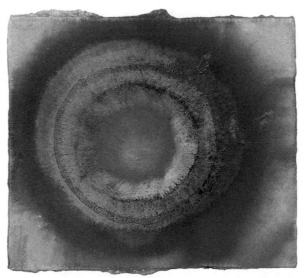

No. XXXIX from *CVIII*, 1985
Watercolor on handmade Pondicherry paper
9⁵/₁₆ x 10¹/₁₆″ (23.7 x 25.6 cm)
Öffentliche Kunstsammlung,
Kupferstichkabinett, Basel

No. LX from *CVIII*, 1985
Watercolor on handmade Pondicherry paper
9³/₄ x 8¹¹/₁₆″ (24.7 x 22.1 cm)
Öffentliche Kunstsammlung,
Kupferstichkabinett, Basel

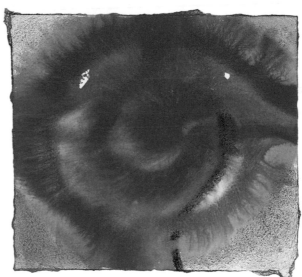

No. CIV from *CVIII*, 1985
Watercolor on handmade Pondicherry paper
9¹/₄ x 10¹/₁₆″ (23.5 x 25.6 cm)
Öffentliche Kunstsammlung,
Kupferstichkabinett, Basel

The Indigo Room, 1983–84
Indigo dye and charcoal with silver attachments on 123 sheets of handmade Pondicherry paper, joined by cotton strips (in four parts)
97⅝ x 235″ (248 x 596.9 cm) to 123¼ x 235″ (313.1 x 596.9 cm)
Anthony d'Offay Gallery, London; Sperone Westwater, New York

The Twenty-four Indian Miniatures

Stella Kramrisch

The twenty-four Indian miniatures by Francesco Clemente were painted in gouache in 1980–81 on sheets of handmade Indian rag paper, about two hundred years old, that were originally the pages of an old book. The book no longer exists. The text that appeared on the pages of the book was wiped off, its easily soluble ink offering no more resistance than does the white chalk on a blackboard. Wiping off the writing of such old manuscripts considered of no particular value and then reusing the cleaned paper has been a common practice. The lines that once framed each panel of text, however, were preserved and reused as the borders of Clemente's miniatures; the wide margins of the pictures have the sheen of old ivory.

Clemente's use of this antique paper authenticated the paintings it was to receive as "Indian." The paintings themselves were to substantiate this claim further if only in accepting the original margins of the pages as their own. The Persian writing still visible in the margins repeats the last word of the text of the respective page and the first word of its continuation on the next page. This was done for the sake of continuity in reading the original manuscript. Clemente's miniatures function as a kind of stepping-stone into the past, since from about the fourteenth century handmade rag paper had served as the ground for book illustrations in India.

The paintings have no name, although one (p. 98 right) bears an inscription. Two of Clemente's paintings suggest that they are the front and back covers of a book, with the one on the "front" (p. 98 left) declaring the authorship of the twenty-four miniatures in bold, Roman characters: FRANCESCO CLEMENTE PINXIT. No name, however, is given to the entire series of paintings nor to the single miniatures with their invented landscapes, charismatic youths, and abstract patterns. The last are also contained in schematic panels between the heavy lettering and a flower border of the introductory painting (p. 98 left). The trompe l'oeil perspective at the top of this image demonstrates that the "book" is a heavy one.

Numerically its twenty-four paintings equal the number of letters in the Greek alphabet, from which the Roman alphabet is derived. All words consist of letters; they transmit the meaning of the text. There being, however, no text to the book, the twenty-four miniatures take its place.

The twenty-four paintings are ideograms. They are not illustrations, and there is no narrative to which they refer. The ideograms each present a situation in a setting of its own. The situation is that of human figures, whole or in parts, in a planar area that evokes either a landscape or a pictorial space construct. The colors mostly are cool and soft, blues, gray, mauve, green, maize, with occasionally a carrot-red or black accent. The figures in the spaces are those of young males. They are mostly naked, lithe of limb. Their faces are bland, dispassionately attractive; they are part of the body. The proportion and physiognomy of the figures are different in each miniature, conveying the sensation, emotion, mood, and thought consonant with the form of each painting. The gestures of the figures carry the action. Precise outlines define each of the figures of the charismatic adolescents, whole or maimed. This definition of the bounding contours of their figures was an abiding trait of Indian miniatures of the sixteenth to seventeenth centuries. In Clemente's paintings, its elastic tenseness isolates the pallor of the naked bodies from the planar ground. Resuscitation, transformation, and reintegration have been at work in Clemente's creations. Landscape and the perspective of Mughal painting as well as the planar spacing of other Indian schools are remembered in his miniatures. Their genealogy is one of conscious choice.

The perspective of the European Renaissance was directly imported to India in the later years of the reign of Emperor Akbar (1556–1605), to whose imperial studio Mughal art owes its splendor. While accepting the complexity of Mughal painting for the settings of his ideograms, Clemente instills into them as the occasion may demand his own rendering of Renaissance perspective that intensifies the spatial suggestiveness of some of the miniatures (pp. 104 left, 107 right, 108 left). The Mughal landscapes and buildings are appropriated in a new context in which they play their part as an accompaniment, a kind of drone to the melody of the new compositions.

The stereotype of the landscape that Clemente has taken over from Mughal paintings consists of a very high horizon line that allows the painted field to retain its planar character. Above this the suggestion of a setting recessed in space, which creates the illusion of three-dimensional reality, is obtained by the introduction of two kinds of schemata in the shape of rocks and buildings. The formula for rocks in Mughal painting had been inherited from Persian paintings, where it had been in turn assimilated from Chinese precedents. The buildings, including fortresses, sanctuaries, and other architectural units, create the illusion of being situated high in the background. Their perspective obeys formulas at home in the tradition of painting in the Eastern churches that were adopted from medieval Western antecedents and that ultimately go back to classical antiquity.

A third motif, ubiquitous in Mughal paintings and faithfully rendered in Clemente's miniatures, is the tufts of vegetation, be they grass, flowers, or shrubs, that are sprinkled in varying density and combinations all over the plane of the paintings, up to the high horizon line. Besides this Mughal landscape with its historical components Clemente has introduced various contemporary components as the building elements in the space constructs of many of the twenty-four miniatures. Although these mainly Islamic idioms were not lying as readily available as was the now-defunct tradition of Indian painting, they were transmuted and adopted from the ancient but still-present patterns of perforated screens, tiled walls, and woven textiles.

In these two kinds of scenarios, whether Mughal landscape or abstract construct, readied from the past of Indian art, the charismatic youths move with grace and decorum, single or in multiples, whole in body or amputated and fragmented, embodiments of apprehensions and sensations of the artist who lavished on them his resources of experience, memory, humor, and grace. The figures move with an elegant spontaneity that does not suggest the next phase their evolution is likely to take. As if under a spell, stasis has ceased them as soon as they were envisioned. Their movements are timeless; they are the last of their respective forms; they are conceptual, abstracted from performance. They are inherent in the cast of the figures in the ideogram presented on the respective page.

These charismatic naked youths of fair complexion, their smooth limbs bounded by sharp yet flowing outlines, are the actors in most of the paintings. Always — with scant exception (p. 102 left) — naked, never aroused sexually, integer in body and limbs or mutilated, the figure of man is pervasively part of the ideogram. Only once does a bovine animal grace the landscape (p. 102 right); only once again the figure of man has grown a tail (p. 106 left), snugly extending as a serpentine appendage that curves from its somnolent owner's body. He is oblivious of the world around him and into which he emits his potential animality while he remains self-contained.

The adolescents who people Clemente's compositions are unlike any figures depicted in the Indian miniatures from which their setting is appropriated. They are the agile actors in most of the paintings, their bland faces are cast in conformity with and as part of the physiognomy of the body; their features carry as much expression as the other parts of their bodies. Where more than one figure is found in a painting, their features resemble one another; they are multiples of one type. Two types of body shapes appear in the scenes. The maimed bodies and their amputated parts are either comparatively chubby, or they are assimilated to the more slender and unfragmented types that inhabit the landscapes of their Mughal antecedents. In one scene (p. 98 right), their diverse features and proportions from a larva-like childhood to maturity dramatize their common lot in a gust of activity, an unrelenting square dance of their common fate. As puppets on a prepared stage, they have been created by Clemente. They play their parts obeying an invisible command.

With a fluid precision of outline akin to that of the figures in illuminations of medieval Indian manuscripts from Bengal or Nepal as well as Mughal and Rajput miniatures, Clemente's figures are set off against the landscape of Mughal provenance in one-half of the paintings. Their trim, thin outlines delimit the figures against their planar ground, in total contrast to Clemente's gouaches, which float on and melt into the surrounding ground.

The settings in which the figures appear, inasmuch as they are appropriations from preexisting works of art, establish a mood of security out of which the pictures emerge as ideograms of utterly new concepts. They are precipitations of visions, experiences, and sensations of Clemente. Their camouflage — their resemblance to Indian miniatures — is a security measure that allows hitherto visually unrecorded experiences to gain a preexisting ambiance. What prompted Francesco Clemente to adopt artistically defunct scenery to function as a backdrop for the play of his figures in a preestablished setting? The Mughal and Rajput conventions of Indian miniature paintings are resuscitated elements for new creations, thematically as well as formally.

A visit to the Jaipur workshop of a contemporary maker of copies and versions of Mughal and Rajput miniatures allowed Clemente to see the method by which this craft was practiced. Here he also found young apprentices, not more than twelve to fifteen years old, who expertly and repetitively filled in the typical details that enliven the traditional landscape setting that is the planar ground in Clemente's miniatures. For heightened credibility the ancient paper with all its blemishes was left untouched, forming a framing margin of the paintings.

The apprentices added these small tufts of vegetation — be they grass or flowers and blossoming trees — in rhythmical sequence according to the needs of the miniature. Clemente chose the size, shape, and spacing of the tufts from the repertory of Mughal painting, and then adjusted them to the context of each of the ideograms he had conceived. In this way the setting over which Clemente's visions would range was prepared. In each case it captured themes hitherto unknown, supporting each in its unique form. Whereas Mughal and Rajput paintings illustrate given themes familiar to their artists, Clemente's mythology is his own; he creates the theme in the form of his vision. His paintings are not illustrations, they are not posterior to any text, although at times they may resonate with the presence of an Indian god or recall a scene in the *Satyricon* of Petronius. Such latent or conscious memories leave their aroma in the paintings of which they have become ingredients.

The artifice of the reshaped Mughal landscape is but one of the scenarios in which Clemente's figures are at home. The other is an abstract setting, a space construct in which the figures are set performing their assigned roles against frames replete with the contradiction of indefinitely extensible repeat patterns such as those of Islamic tiles and textiles, which create the effect of superimposed transparencies and alternating identities (pp. 98 right, 101 right). By the stasis of their gestures, even at their liveliest the figures incorporate the motionless, immovable units of pattern in front of which they manifest (p. 99 left).

Just as there are these two kinds of settings — the transposed "naturalistic," open-air space of the Mughal type on the one hand, and the abstract space construct on the other — there are also two types of figures — those who are whole in body and those who are fragmented,

Figure 33. Francesco Clemente
Cover of Michael Auping, *Francesco Clemente*
(New York: Harry N. Abrams, Inc., 1985)

truncated, amputated. Both types are at ease within their condition; unimpeded, the dance of the amputated is joyous (p. 99 left). Their bland, nearly identical faces take no cognizance of the mutilation of their bodies, and the dance goes on, its rhythmic ease choreographed on the geometrical pattern of the painted field. Or the amputated parts exist by themselves, each having a movement or position of their own in the complex web of pattern of one of the paintings (p. 99 right).

Multiple ambiguity connects the figures with their abstract ground. Planar, it is the backdrop behind the performance of the manikins whose evolutions are directed by an invisible puppeteer (p. 99 left). Overlaid by strips and planes, it is the space in which their gyrations are playful impossibilities acted out in a vacuum on treacherous planks threatened with immediate collapse although upheld, it would appear, from above by the flagstaffs held by the figures (p. 98 right). Ambiguously and precariously the staffs seem to rest on the patterned planks on which the figures perform. The three large flags fluttering vehemently high above the performers are inscribed *Naufragium est* (The shipwreck is [everywhere]),[1] *abiit ad plures* (He is gone to the many),[2] and *homo bulla* (man [is] an ephemeral bubble).[3] While the fourth flag carries no message, its operator appears on his way to "the many," where he is seen once more, collapsing further down.

The anguished commotion of the wavers of the flags with their macabre inscriptions is such that it makes the carriers leap and soar. They are young, jumping as they hold on to their flagstaffs with one hand while the other wields a gun. The gun is the inalienable attribute of each of the flagholders, but only one of them triggers it.

The life-death tension of the shipwreck keeps the merry-go-round moving. It is the ambiguity of this painting that determined its spatial structure. The figures swing along in the ambiguity of their entanglement as they hold on to the staffs that they also hold aloft, their ambiguous performance whirling in the direction of the one who has "gone to the many." Sinking, he bends over a fallen flag.

In another painting (p. 99 left) beauteous figures perform in front of a patterned ground, mastering their movements. Although they are all alike, each is motivated specifically by the lack of either one limb, or two, or three. The precariousness of the single dancer, bereft of one limb or the other, is absorbed in the arabesque of rhythmically repeated identical movements that identifies each figure as being also the other. Each balding manikin dances with the same grace in a composition of intersecting diagonals of which each dancer, although not whole, is wholly part, unaware of his fragmentation. If fragmentation and lack of completeness are conditions inwardly experienced in contemporary life, they are here neatly delineated. In contrast to this introspective provenance, a painterly origin of the incomplete limbs equally carries visual momentum. In some of Clemente's works (Figure 33), the completeness of the composition is carried by the position of the truncated limb, which is suggested by only as much of the limb as needed to convey the impetus of the gesture. An explicitly drawn limb would in this case be redundant. Fragmentation is thus both an inwardly experienced state of awareness and a pictorial device that combine in this painting of the dancers (p. 99 left).

In another miniature (p. 99 right), the amputated limbs and the truncated body as well as the severed head are seen finding their places in a conjunction of three indefinitely expandable patterns. The interlinked hexagonal pattern in the middle of the composition suggests the movement of the waves of a river. It flows between shores of patterned fabric where severed limbs, including trunk and heads, float, disappear, and emerge; there is no hold anywhere. It seems easy to check the amputated parts, which are scattered in readiness for being assembled. Caprice and wit present them as if in motion. They are parts of an ideogram swiftly

Figure 34. Francesco Clemente
One, 1985
Gouache on handmade paper, 94 x 94" (238.8 x 238.8 cm)
Courtesy Sperone Westwater, New York

passing through the mind, seen while being painted on the backdrop curtain of more than one layer and thickness.

The scurrilous activity of the amputated body parts drowning and emerging is remedied by the ingenuity of the planar layout and its associated thought allowing for several conjunctions: of firm land on both banks, the farther bank, however, also rising abruptly, with a corporate building encroached upon by truncated body parts searching for help and being trapped. In their dehumanization the several body parts are part of an outcry made visible.

Of special importance to Clemente is the theme of the hand, its fingers in particular (p. 100 left; see also pp. 63, 79, 176–77). Its index finger raised, the thumb bent in a strident angle over two other bent fingers, draw attention to the little finger whose tip is amputated, a triple stream of blood gushing from it. Below the hand and on the same backdrop with its minutely granulated allover floral pattern, the amputated tip hovers horizontally. A stream of blood gushes from the wound and finds its way down to earth in a pool.

The gesture of this large, enigmatic hand is known to no ritual, neither Indian nor Christian.[4] The harsh angle of the bent thumb augments its portentous character. It would seem as if the nemesis of amputation has raised a warning finger that refers to the actual practice — by the Mafia — of severing the tip of the little finger as a punishment for and deterrent of fraudulent action.

The theme of the cut-off finger recurs in Clemente's gouache *One* (Figure 34). There the forefinger is similarly maimed, while in *The Four Corners* (p. 79), the entire hand, its fingers intact, exhibits the whole world extended over the palm and fingers. The play of numbers from one to five has its support in the fingers of the hand, whether they are whole or amputated in part. It would seem that the number of fingers, whole or fragmented, is associated with the number of sense organs and the wholeness of the five-fingered hand comprising the entire world. The hand, most ancient of body symbols in the world of art, is varied by Clemente with portentous actuality.

Different from the solitary weightiness of the hand is a busy landscape in which a maimed torso strides across a landscape under a radiant moon and star-studded sky (p. 100 right). There is also a large fish — as if abandoned by Klee — surpassing in size a kite-fish that the spool-child or cocoon-child in its kiosk lets fly; the kite-fish is no rival to the big fish, yet is capable of soaring higher than the large fish, the flag, and the moon. This celebration of childhood is guarded in the four directions by four cranes or storks (it is the stork that in European folklore delivers the child into the world) where it will grow and — amputated — stride along to enjoy the luscious fruits that nature keeps ready for him in a basket. Or, having lost his left arm (p. 101 left), man in all four directions eagerly holds up a telescope to scan the luminary that appears thrice, if only to be an easier target, amidst a galaxy of stars sprinkled over the amputated trunk of Cosmic Man laid out gigantically above the plant-tufted ground of the earth. The visionary power of the cosmic torso rules over the eager concentration of the four star watchers from an imperfect world that does not provide for all. Star-spangled Cosmic Man truncated forms the ground on which one-armed astronomers direct their telescopes like the players on a billiard table on which the luminaries are the billiard balls. Superimposed ideograms, seen in a flash and abiding as an image, create a new perspective of above and below.

Cosmic Man, star studded like the Milky Way in Clemente's miniature painting, has a powerful antecedent in a preparatory study of about 1950 by Marcel Duchamp, done in gouache on transparent plexiglass.[5] It represents a truncated female body studded with dotlike perforations that define and enhance the modeling of the majestic female body in motion. Yet even when man is in possession of his unmutilated self he is exposed to vicissitudes for which he may or may not be prepared.

Man as an integer stands erect, looking up to a large and ambiguous umbrella transparently open in a context in which the strong vertical of its handle acts as a measuring stick of a world of ambiguity (p. 101 right). It is paper thin, deceptively planar, a construct of overlapping patterned, transparent fields whose density ambiguously shifts from picture ground to object. The sharp-edged corner of the folded-over, paper-thin patterned ground heralds the game being played by the unfurled umbrella exchanging inside and outside, coalescing them as they overlap. In this precarious situation man — perhaps holding a double whisk — stands firm and erect in three-quarter back view, his noble head in profile looking up to the balance of incongruous moieties.

Abstract planar patterns asserting themselves one against the other are assigned their roles by the handle of the umbrella held high with unswerving attention by the naked figure of man. As a sheer construct of patterned planes, the painting is a symbol of man in the universe. Figures like the fish (p. 105 left) or the hand (p. 100 left) represent verbal, conceptual symbols. Their ancient, established meaning is drawn into a pictorial context, conceived by Clemente, that shows forth further, specific significance.

Different from these preexistent and universal figurative symbols are the nonconceptual forms arising from the craft of drawing itself, patterns without a name ordered according to the dynamism of becoming symbols in their own context, engendering patterns that act on one another as they fill the page in a context peculiar to the particular page and not repeated elsewhere (p. 101 right).

Resorting, however, to the chosen ambiance of an extinguished Mughal scenario, this background is resuscitated, appropriated, and charged with new contents. They provide a setting that distances sensorial experiences from the embarrassment of their immediacy (pp. 102 left, 107 left). Sensations and memories drift across or commingle in the ideograms that have the Mughal landscape setting for their actualization (p. 102 left and right).

Near the top of a flower-tufted plane of the ground and on its horizon line a man practices a kind of *shīrsha āsana*, the yogic headstand (p. 102 left). In it, according to tradition, the subtle, vital breath is carried toward the head by the movement of the blood. The process awakens the subtle, vital, coiled energy (*kuṇḍalinī*). The yoga practitioner in the painting relaxes; his legs do not rise straight, they are crossed. Another figure standing higher up on the horizon line bends in a scissor-sharp angle from the hip joint, while he sniffs at the toes of the yoga practitioner's right foot, gazing at his left foot that holds up a flower. Both men wear shorts, the only pieces of garment worn by any figure in a landscape painting. The playful crossing of the representation of an embodied concept (yoga) with an enactment of sensory experience is made possible by the artifice of the landscape in which it takes place.

A more comprehensive amalgam of traditional Indian themes within Clemente's version is achieved in a picture of spring (p. 102 right), where, according to traditional Indian poetry, black bees and parrots are messengers of both the season and love.[6] Besieged with a swarm of oversized bees, their victim protects himself in a nearby grove that with its densely foliated trees shields him, on whose head a parrot — another symbol of vernal love — has perched for good measure, as he relieves himself from this onslaught of love symbols by throwing up a mighty jet of vomit. Above all this misspent bounty a solitary cow paces along on the verdant, flower-speckled ground. These scenes of humorous assimilation of given Indian concepts are as full of new thematic conjunctions as they are of pictorial consistency.

Other paintings fill a richer Mughal landscape setting with emotion rather than with sensory experience (p. 103 left and right). Thus the paraphernalia of the readjusted Mughal scenario become witness of a scene of frustration in which a youth pleadingly addresses a school of fish who steadfastly and heedlessly swim away with staring eye (p. 103 left). (The fish are here in their element, the water, where their silent criticism is on the social and psychological plane. Moreover, in Clemente's work, the fish has cosmic dimension, functioning as the *axis mundi* while also retaining its sociological implications [p. 105 left].) Although there is no witness near the pond, where the youth addresses the fish, high up on the distant mountains a stalwart trumpeter blows forth the news for the inhabitants of the fortified castle across the hills to hear.

This scene of frustration and apprehension gives way in another painting to a riverine idyll (p. 103 right). A river flows calmly at the foot of a low mountain range crested by dark buildings. On the further bank of the river a long-limbed youth reclines. A spurt of water springs forth in a wide arch from his head and ensconces his slender, lying body. The jet of water falls into the broad stream that it has engendered for a youth, his alter ego and like himself, to bathe in, as fish frolic around his refreshed person. There is no greater joy than to be immersed and carried by the waters of creation, one's own creative power flowing from one's head with calm assurance. This ideogram recalls an Indian myth in visual terms that entirely become Clemente's own.

Shiva, the Great God, received on his head the onslaught of the celestial river Ganges as she descended from the empyrean down to earth. She rested for a while in the ascetic god's matted strands of hair, and then flowed to earth to fertilize its lands and minds.

In some Indian miniatures that have the Descent of the Ganges for their theme, the River is shown at the moment of leaving her divine although temporary station on Shiva's head, the preceding part of the myth being implied but not illustrated. Clemente's reclining youth (p. 103 right) allows the River to originate from his head, relaxedly recapitulating the myth in his own person.

The great mythical themes of India reverberate in other of Clemente's ideograms. God is an archer when his name is Desire (*kāma*/*eros*). In Clemente's miniature he is singled out from the landscape receding far into the distance (p. 104 left). He occupies the center of the painting, with his arrow ready to fly but his target unshown. Alone, his noble figure commands the wide terrace. Outside in the distance two identical youths appear in a landscape in which the hillside has burst into flowers and the distant mountain ranges skirt high sanctuaries under a sky astir with delicate swirls of clouds that have traveled from the Far East. The youths stand ready, phantomlike, raising an arm as if saluting, while they seem to be carried on the spokes of an invisible Ferris wheel. They are recurring, ready targets, as are the flowering branches in front of them. They are the ever-renewed victims of the god, but he does not aim at them. He is an emblem of their destiny. His taut bow is timelessly about to be discharged.

Visual impressions stored in different moments of experience and activated from their state of latency commingle with recollections and recognitions. They crystallize and emerge as one coherent theme sanctioned by tradition and brought to life once more. The large tree, the cosmic axis, the world tree, the tree of Jesse, the nameless tree, spontaneously grown and somewhat off center, rises here from the supine body of man as a naked youth, resting his head on his right arm (p. 104 right). He looks up from the flowery ground of this world and raises his left arm to point to the top of the tree where *ecce homo*, his alter ego, reclines on his side, his head similarly supported as that of his double below, and his left arm resting on his body. Man below is both the place of origin of the tree and the support of man above resting in its dense foliage. The tree growing from the middle of the body of supine man in medieval Western art is a symbol of transformation, of birth following death.

In a purely Indian synthesis of conceptions, the images of the cosmic axis and the myth of the fish incarnation of god Vishnu combine as an elegant fish-amphora risen from the terrace (p. 105 left). Man as above so below has here assumed different gender and allure. The seductive figure below is that of an elegant woman reclining with the supporting help of a tabouret, while her body is traversed by the stem of the amphora. Her disinterested counterpart in the shape of man — older than the youthful performers in the other mythic contexts — is shown above absorbed in practicing a yoga exercise near the corner of the gaping mouth of the fish-amphora. The bleak stare of the one jutting eye of the fish, its stiff fin-shaped handles, the spreading drapery of its tail, and the scales of its body seem to define the vessel as made of porcelain, opening its huge mouth in agonized emptiness. The world of the idle rich sustained by accepted concepts of the culture that enable them to hold their position graces the complexity of this hieratic — and humorous — composition. It extends upward to a rich architectural assortment above a horizontal mountain screen, most distantly descended from its Mughal antecedents.

Whole or maimed, Clemente's figures of man as gently playful adolescents, either wholly engaged in their presence or whimsically complaisant in their afflictions, know no violence except in one instance, where a form so large that it practically exceeds the size of the painting bursts forth emitting glowing, red-hot darts and twisted flames or petals (p. 105 right). The violence of this sunburst has no end; it emanates from a circle bounded by a ring of unmelting metal around a stippled flowery plane undisturbed by the explosion around it. With great speed the small figure of a burly youth comes running, wielding scissors larger than himself. Undaunted, he is about to cut the shooting darts and flames, a superhuman task. But as yet the scissors are still open, and the twisting flame-petals dart undisturbed. In its power this vision surpasses the tranquil introspection that makes the other miniatures spirited or serenely scurrilous ideograms. The heroic-pathetic self-set task of the wielder of the scissors, his figure almost unnoticeable against the formidable burst of flames that fills the entire painting, wants to be seen as opposite to that of the holder of the umbrella (p. 101 right), the master over ambivalence, the upholder of balance in this world.

However, these are not the only possibilities for action within the human condition. Attentively, leisurely, and not far from sleep, the time has come in the well-being of a summer afternoon for a tail to grow unseen and barely felt by the now somnolent youth (p. 106 left). Below, his awakened figure sits up on a carpet in a state of wonderment. (Clemente has said that he first intended to equip this figure with the tail.)

At such times, in fact at any time, bodily sensations may take over, and their images are recorded in the landscape and buildings in which Clemente's figures dwell. An act of hitherto unrecorded hermaphroditism or procreative bisexuality has its exponent in the figure of man, seen in back view, heavy of body and coarse of mien, no longer a youth, who is capable of having emitted an egg that he can cook and serve without a change of position, leaving it not uncertain from which orifice the egg was produced (p. 106 right). The body of this burly man seated on the floor of the terrace is a boiler whence he gathers and serves the egg — hot — on a spoon, while his still-hot body spurts from the mouth a hissing jet of liquid across the balustrade of the terrace and into the landscape. The emissions from the body's orifices thus enrich the terrace as well as the landscape. On the left, the man's glance in profile vaults over the spurt of liquid; on the right, his arm reaches backward to serve the egg from the spoon into the empty bowl ready to receive it.

Furthermore, a surrealistic conflation with its anal implication is rendered in another painting (p. 107 left), where the cut-off lower half of a squatting male body — on top of the world — fills the flower-dotted hillside with its invisible gaseous emission that has made the flowers on the world hillside recede. Only the hardy, small tufts of grass could stay put. The Mughal floral pattern denoting and evoking nature, a convention of courtly painting, has been disturbed by the unprecedented subject matter of this painting. The emission is inhaled in ecstatic distortion by two acolytes, whose bodies it inflates at the foot of the hill.

The privilege of the male emitting an egg is further extended by having the egg placed at his feet (p. 107 right). It now has also the shape of a fruit or lotus bud, as the man holds it in each of his hands surmounting his shoulders, alike to Sūrya, the Indian sun god whose icon holds lotus flowers in a similar gesture. The man's legs are stretched inordinately as if in the process of growing from the egg shape below toward the two egg-buds flanking his head. The landscape behind this man on the terrace leads into a depth that is barely Mughal, the tiled rather than carpeted terrace emphasizing the tension between nature and culture that is resolved by the figure of man as the bond in common.

Standing on the terrace of his house, thinking, undecided, insecure, and on stiff legs, man holds a long-stemmed flower (p. 108 left). But instead of smelling it he appears to close his nostrils, for as shown in another miniature (p. 107 left), the inhalation of smell shapes and distorts body physiognomies into those of bizarre characters.

Even so, and however maimed and ambivalent, his arms amputated, his feet like those of a specter facing back, man undergoes an apotheosis (p. 108 right). Standing high up on the vast verdant mountain slope of the world, snow-capped by distant Himalayan ranges, he commands the scene as he turns his head in profile. Bundles of rays of high tension sprout as wings from his averted, armless chest, and an enormous stream colored deep carrot-red flows from his penis. As its waves traverse the acid-green mountainside, the stream takes its course behind a preternaturally large telephone and, forming a loop, passes out of the painting.

However, no message will be heard by one whose ears and mouth are muzzled, and whose eyes are shielded (p. 109 left). All these aids for closing off and protecting the sense organs add to the sterility of fully clothed and burly man, loaded with the paraphernalia of office. Behind and above him naked man strides on stilts, his phantom presence almost about to enclose the muzzled man in the pincerlike grip of the stilts.

The painting on the back "cover" of the "book" (p. 109 right) is divided into two halves of contrasting colors. Each half has also an indefinitely extensible design that covers its entire extent. In the middle the two halves interlock. Color and design of the upper rectangle fill also the half-circle of the lower half. For good balance the meeting of rectangle and half-circle appear once more within the field of each half of the page. There, at the upper and lower edge respectively of each of the rectangular half-pages, a small rectangle is inserted, capped by a circular device. Both together form a new unit patterned by one or more indefinitely extensible designs. The entire small complex appears like a domed building rising from its own ground in monumental simplicity. It brings to a close the multifaceted contents of the book.

The front and back "covers" of the "book" (pp. 98 left, 109 right) show a ponderous sobriety that has its figurative exponent in the muzzled man (p. 109 left). In painting the spirited stilt walker, naked, phantomlike, and yet *integer vitae* although stilt borne, is twice unseen by the voluminous muzzled man, who faces away from the apparition on the flowery mountain meadow but could not, his eyes being covered, see the soaring apparition even if he tried.

The telephone (p. 108 right), the muzzled man, the front and back "covers" are metaphors of the outer world, which, in its present concrete actuality, is a heavy load to bear.

1. From the lament over the shipwrecked body of Lychas and the frailty of man as told by Petronius in his *Satyricon* (12.115).

2. *Satyricon* (5.42).

3. Ibid. The actual phrase in the text is *nos non pluris sumus quam bullae* (We are nothing but bubbles).

4. The hand is of greatest importance in Clemente's works; many paintings with the theme appear in publications that were issued after the writing of this essay, which occurred in 1987 without any verbal communication with the artist.

5. See Anne d'Harnoncourt and Walter Hopps, *Etant Donnés: 1° la chute d'eau, 2° le gaz d'éclairage: Reflections on a New Work by Marcel Duchamp* (Philadelphia, 1973), reissued as a revised edition of the *Philadelphia Museum of Art Bulletin*, vol. 64, nos. 299–300 (April–September 1969), p. 10, fig. 3, and esp. p. 62, fig. 41.

6. Daniel H. H. Ingalls, *An Anthology of Sanskrit Court Poetry* (Cambridge, Mass., 1965), p. 113, no. 157.

Francesco Clemente Pinxit, 1980–81
Series of twenty-four paintings in gouache on
antique handmade Indian rag paper
each 8¾ x 6″ (22.2 x 15.2 cm)
Virginia Museum of Fine Arts, Richmond.
Gift of Sydney and Frances Lewis

 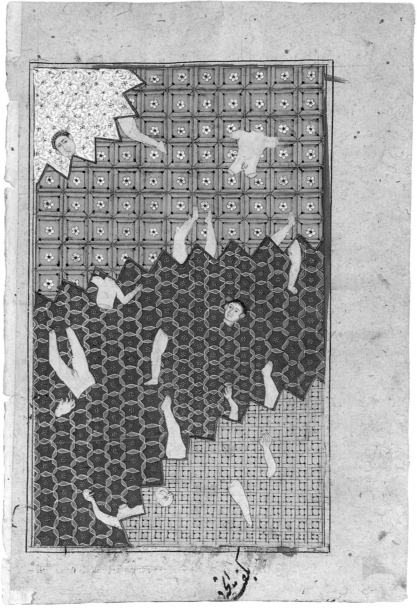

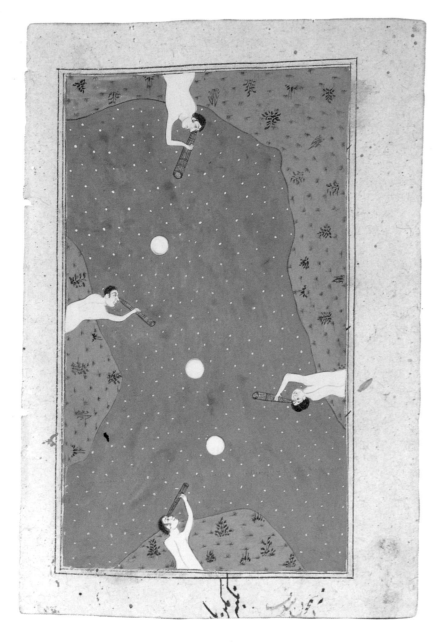

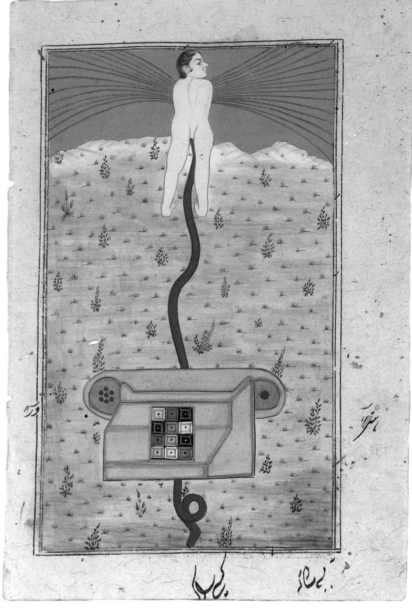

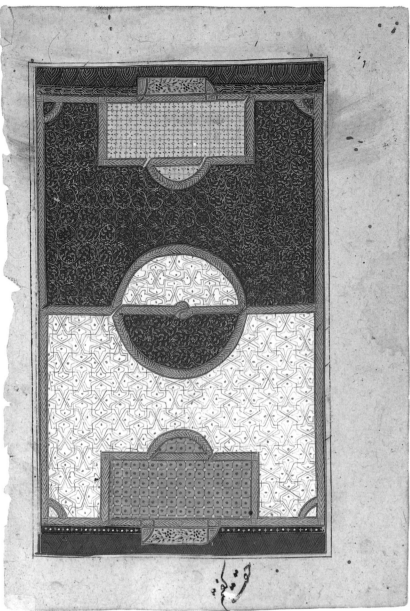

New York

Francesco Clemente, Blake-inspired painter, looking over handcut
Album with new poem I'd scribed out for him to watercolor illum-
inate, our third book so prepared. He liked this picture, corner of
his studio loft overlooking Great Jones Street Manhattan, october 1984.
Allen Ginsberg

New York

Raymond Foye

Art is the only twin life has—its only valid metaphysic. Art does not seek to describe but to enact. And if man is once more to possess intent in his life, and to take up the responsibility implicit in his life, he has to comprehend his own process as intact, from outside, by way of his skin, in, and by his own powers of conversion, out again.
            Charles Olson[1]

From the start New York has held for Francesco Clemente a mythic allure as a city precariously balanced between the two poles of his young life: East and West. Whereas Rome offered a deep repositorium of history and culture, and India a complex tapestry of religion and myth, New York represented the possibility of a new beginning, where the experiences of the past could be synthesized into something entirely new. Clemente's first, month-long visit to New York, in March of 1981, convinced him to return to the city early in 1982 with his wife and two daughters, to set up a permanent studio and home.

Within a few weeks of settling in New York, in one of those odd happenstances of cultural dislocation that seem to shadow him, Clemente discovered just to the east of his studio a tiny storefront ashram dedicated to his favorite guru, Ramana Maharshi. Immediately to the west were the neighborhoods of Greenwich Village, filled with the cafés of Little Italy, newsstands, and grocery stores, as well as Roman Catholic churches dedicated to the patron saints of Naples and Amalfi. A few weeks later he and his wife discovered a Hindu temple in Queens, built by stonemasons from Madras and dedicated to Ganesha.

Awash in diversity and decay, New York is a city where styles and modes are abruptly juxtaposed and combined. The vast array of nationalities and language groups that coexist in New York offer a staggering cross section of world culture: over two hundred languages are spoken and more than forty foreign-language newspapers are published there. A plurality of cultures, languages, and religions overlap and intermingle. Standing at the crossroads of world trade, migration, and social mobility, it is a city of acculturation, adaptation, and alienation, three themes that are continually expressed and intertwined in Clemente's work.

It has been a long-held truism in the West that culture is not the product of individual countries or nationalities, but rather of cosmopolitan centers: Rome, London, Paris, Prague, Vienna—New York. Each in its day was a center of artistic and literary ferment, attracting artists and writers of diverse nationalities and backgrounds. New York City in the second half of the twentieth century clearly has occupied such a position. Indeed, it was this cosmopolitan aspect of the city that first attracted Clemente.

Clemente quickly recognized in New York the condition of fragmentation and cultural overlay that had existed in the Rome of Apuleius's *Golden Ass* and Petronius's *Satyricon*, an era known as late antiquity, which he had once characterized thusly: "This was one of the periods when there was a kind of world culture. The world was at the same time one and totally split in a thousand different possibilities. You could find Egyptian people painting Greek pictures, Greeks singing Latin songs, and Latins praying to Eastern gods. By the way, the classical culture the Renaissance knew was this one, the late antique one."[2] New York came to symbolize for Clemente a modern-day counterpart to ancient Rome of the first and second centuries, the seat of a decaying empire where a myriad of cultural strains and diversities coexisted in a simultaneity of styles and systems that reinforced his own complex sense of reality.

Clemente immediately felt at home in this new environment: New York possessed the same squalor and liveliness that the artist had become accustomed to in Naples and Madras, with the added feature of a few hundred all-night restaurants, dance clubs, night spots, and after-

Figure 35. John Lurie, Francesco Clemente, and Jean Michel Basquiat (left to right), photo booth portrait, Area nightclub, New York, 1985

hours bars. Through its sheer size the city offered anonymity—always an important factor for Clemente—combined with an intense, free-floating energy that the artist could plug into as he desired and that suited his enormous capacity for work.

Amidst the environment of urban decay and disillusionment in New York in the late 1970s, the arts in the city took on a force and intensity that recalled the vitality of the 1950s or 1960s. What had been turning out to be amongst the most unexciting decades in recent history unexpectedly gave way to a burgeoning punk rock scene, which in turn provided the meeting ground for the young musicians, film makers, writers, and painters who spawned the "New Wave." Like the 1960s, it was a time of great creativity and cross-fertilization in the arts, when established barriers were torn down and definitions redrawn. Painting, poetry, experimental theater, underground film, fashion, and popular music all seemed to exist, once again, on the same ideal plane of inspired invention. Yet unlike Pop Art of the 1960s, which remained fundamentally a fine art movement, the New York art world of the late 1970s and early 1980s represented a genuine blend of "high" and "low" culture, to the extent that such artificial distinctions lost all meaning.

It was an extraordinary amalgam of urban culture, something which Clemente had been unsuccessfully searching for all through his Rome years, and he responded strongly to the collective vitality of the scene, in particular the exposure it afforded him to the black culture of New York, which he especially revered. In many ways it was the connection to black culture that most affected Clemente in his initial years in New York. He was introduced to the Apollo Theatre and the restaurants and nightclubs of Harlem by the artist Jean Michel Basquiat (Figure 35) and *Interview* magazine editor Paige Powell. He spent many evenings walking the streets of the city alone, into the early morning hours, protected by that shield of safety that so often seems to surround newcomers. Suddenly he felt free of the weight of European historicism that so sapped the creative will.

New York City also provided Clemente with the example of a vital society of working artists, something he had long since despaired of finding in Rome. For the first time in his life he felt a part of a milieu made up of painters, graffiti artists, composers, film makers, poets, and critics. It was a true community of kindred spirits, and Clemente responded enthusiastically, painting and drawing during the afternoon and early evening, and touring the clubs from late night to daybreak. In contrast to Rome, a lack of self-consciousness pervaded the New York art community. There was a casualness and ease with which artists participated in the common idioms of contemporary culture: studio, café, nightclub, gallery. In Rome people were *talking* about doing things; in New York they were actually *doing* them. There was little use or tolerance in New York for the excessive intellectualizing that had become the norm in European art circles. Critics and intellectuals were part of the New York scene, but they did not dominate in disproportionate numbers or influence. Clemente had long since wearied of the hypocrisy of the many European intellectuals who had fashioned a world of self-indulgent criticism that failed or succeeded solely on the rhetorical merits of the discourse, without regard for the actual creative products of painting, poem, or novel. As an artist who had been struggling for nearly a decade to place once again the emphasis in art on emotion and experience, it was a welcomed change. In a published dialogue with the painter Alex Katz, Clemente defended his condemnation of the European intellectual orthodoxy:

> I see artists in America making choices, but they do not declare them as such. True, the choices don't resonate in society because there is no criticism nor debate, although, distinctly, choices are made. In Europe everything is food for debate, but the artists are not necessarily making the tough choices. . . . The European intellectual audience have their ideas nicely lined-up, and they walk around paintings ignoring them, and if there isn't a debate about the choices of the artist, then the intellectuals can be extremely radical without anybody paying a price.[3]

Figure 36. Metal trunk with devotional objects and souvenirs in Clemente's New York studio, 1986

Figure 37. Clemente holding a saint's relic, New York, 1988

Figure 38. Francesco and Alba Clemente in the New York studio, 1988; photographed by Allen Ginsberg

Toward the end of 1982 Clemente established a studio on lower Broadway that he occupies to this day. It is a vast loft that stretches nearly a city block in one direction and one-half block in the other. Inside the studio, visitors were confronted with a decidedly un-New York environment, resembling something of a cross between a Roman catacomb and Hindu shrine. The studio was nearly always kept in the dark and the air was laden with heavy South Indian incense, while a seemingly never-ending succession of Buddhist monks chanted in low drones on the phonograph. Around the perimeter of the studio paintings were precariously propped up against the walls, jutting out at an uncomfortable forty-five-degree angle that lent a sense of anthropomorphic foreshortening to each canvas. On the floor in the center of the studio lay a foot-high pile of several thousand drawings, approximately three-quarters of his output from the previous ten years. Clemente would work almost exclusively on the floor of his studio, with canvases laid out flatly horizontal, and series of drawings or pastels spread out in groups of twelve or more.

Having moved himself and his family into the midst of an unfamiliar and chaotic city, one can speculate that Clemente then sought to create a familiar haven within his studio, bringing with him some of the familiar vestiges of his studios in Rome and Madras. In time the more funereal aspects of the decor fell away; the large swaths of Indian muslin were taken down from the windows, light was admitted, and the studio began to reflect more of the city. Soon Clemente began foraging in the empty lots in his neighborhood (the same lots that Robert Rauschenberg had scoured twenty years earlier for assemblage material), carrying home such finds as rusted bicycle wheels and broken building ornaments. These were spread out on the floor and eventually functioned as sculptural elements or as surfaces on which frescoes were executed. In this respect Clemente was once again resuming his familiar habit of seeking out those materials closest at hand—all the better if discredited or discarded—balanced as his art is between interior experience and the actuality of his surroundings. In the years since 1983 the character of the New York studio has changed greatly in relation to the work that is being produced, but there remains a persistent air of exoticism in the many relics, icons, devotional objects, prayerbooks, fabrics, postcards, toys, and ephemera that are arranged in altarlike configurations in corners, or on metal trunks or small tabletops (Figures 36, 37).

During Clemente's first two years in New York the studio was always open for friends to drop by to converse, view work, and sit for portraits. After an initial greeting Clemente would most often resume work, while his wife Alba would befriend and feed their various guests (Figure 38). The critics Edit deAk or Diego Cortez would spend long afternoons, while Rene Ricard would hold forth on painting and opera, or sit quietly in a corner scribbling poetry. The musicians John Lurie or Airto Lindsay would sometimes hold open rehearsals, or the composer Morton Feldman would drop by. The painters Jean Michel Basquiat, Keith Haring, Brice Marden, Kenny Scharf, and Julian Schnabel were also frequent visitors. Local graffiti artists such as Rammellzee, Lee Quinones, Futura, or Fred Brathwaite were particularly welcome, not only for their humor and refreshing street savvy, but also because of the respect Clemente had for their work. A spontaneous phenomenon of urban life, graffiti writers invented their own language—gestural, automatic, and calligraphic—based on actual script but carried to the point of abstraction. These imaginary inscriptions appealed to Clemente's love of signs, symbols, and pictograms of all types, as well as to his penchant for arcane or imaginary systems devised for transmitting meaning.

Clemente often refers to 1983 as a crucial year in New York, a peak moment when artists, poets, writers, and musicians shared in a remarkable consummation of energy and creativity. Shortly thereafter the sense of comradery began to fall away, due in part to a natural dissipation of energy and in part to the inclination of most artists to declare their own private territory, to separate themselves from a collective movement that may have united one with

Figure 39. Francesco Clemente
Portrait of Keith Haring, 1989
Watercolor on paper, 14 x 17" (35.6 x 43.2 cm)
Collection of Francesco and Alba Clemente, New York

another solely on the basis of their being in the same place at the same time. Undoubtedly the encroachment of money and publicity took its toll, separating the commercially successful artists from the unsuccessful ones, and in general alienating artists from the fellowship they had once shared. Yet it was also a matter of just getting down to work; a great many artists had coasted along using the "New Wave" and "Neo-Expressionist" appellations, and the time had come to separate those who had something to offer from those who merely reflected or reacted to the hyperboles of the day. By early 1984 Clemente had retreated into his studio to resume the workaday life style to which he had become accustomed in Madras and Rome.

Although visitors became fewer, a steady stream of friends and acquaintances continued to stop by the studio, and they are recorded in the open-ended series of watercolor portraits that the artist has been working on since 1982 (Figure 39). Clemente's skills as a portraitist are best revealed in these works, as are his talents as a watercolorist. By selecting a medium that forbids reworkings or revisions, he forces himself to capture with freshness his immediate impressions of the sitter before him. They show the artist at his most hesitant and vulnerable, and are unique in his *oeuvre* in that they are strictly depictive of what he sees in front of him, divested of the myths, symbols, or metaphors so often employed. Each sitter is depicted frontally, stripped of any posture of guardedness or self-assurance. The quiet power of these works derives from the intense gaze that seems to unite artist and sitter.

The importance of materials to Clemente cannot be overestimated, since in his view the work is as much a product of what it is made of as how or why it is made. His approach is intensely physical and reveals an intuitive respect for the integral nature of the mediums. Materials are what they are: pastels are dry and chalky; watercolors are thin and fluid; pen and ink drawings are starkly scratched. The power that the viewer experiences in his work is based as much in this elemental sense of materials as in the intellectual process behind the art. Earth, air, fire, water—these are the primal forces latent in the materials Clemente uses; his preference is for dried pigments, dug from the earth and applied with a minimum of medium, usually a small amount of transparent glue used as binding. In papers he chooses the thick Indian sheets molded from heavy cotton pulp or the exceedingly thin Japanese rice papers, whose translucent structure reveals both the material and its making. The prototypes for many of his sculptures (see p. 78) were fashioned in Madras in papier-mâché and caked with earth, only to be transformed by fire into bronze and copper sculptures. Indeed, it is unlikely that Clemente could range as far and wide as he does in subjects and ideas were his objects not rooted in the visceral facts of their making.

For all of the confusion and squalor outside, the New York studio became a place of quiet stasis, a laboratory in which Clemente could settle down and begin one of the most industrious phases of his career. Chiefly, New York influenced Clemente temperamentally; its hold on him was not fundamentally as a source of subject matter, in the way that Madras or Rome had left their marks in so many identifiable ways on the impressionable young artist. Instead New York has functioned more as a sympathetic place of neutrality and anonymity, where he could be left to his own devices and disinterested contemplation. Like the other locales, New York became a tool, the milieu through which he could channel his work. In this sense Clemente uses geography as medium, the way other painters use paint or canvas. Although he arrived in New York after he had fully developed his mature style, his general attitude of openness and vulnerability led to instances in which Clemente's work does show the influence of the visual legacy of the New York School, firstly in the example of the Abstract Expressionists, and secondly in the example of Andy Warhol.

Figure 40. Francesco Clemente
No. XI, from the series *The Fourteen Stations,* 1982–83
Oil on canvas, 78 x 93″ (198.1 x 236.2 cm)
Courtesy Thomas Ammann, Zurich

Figure 41. Willem de Kooning
(American, born Holland, 1904)
Woman II, 1952
Oil on canvas, 59 x 43″ (149.9 x 109.2 cm)
The Museum of Modern Art, New York.
Gift of Mrs. John D. Rockefeller 3rd

Figure 42. Francesco Clemente
Untitled, 1983
Oil on canvas, 82 x 28″ (208.3 x 71.1 cm)
Courtesy Sperone Westwater, New York

In the latter part of 1982, when Clemente first established his studio on lower Broadway, he set about work on two successive series of paintings, *The Midnight Sun* (1982) and *The Fourteen Stations* (1982–83).[4] These were the first significant works he produced in New York, and both show at least a subconscious engagement of Abstract Expressionism. In *The Midnight Sun,* Clemente is painting in oils for the first time, using a freely gestural approach in contradistinction to the seemingly languorous execution and faded surfaces that recall the frescoes of southern Italy and are so often found in his Roman works. In *The Fourteen Stations* (Figure 40), he shows a similar dynamic energy, coupled with a complex layering of imagery strongly akin to that of Willem de Kooning, a painter whose work Clemente had carefully studied at this time in a large retrospective exhibition in Stockholm (Figures 41, 42).[5] Partly because of these works and partly because of the tendency of the art press to clamor after convenient "isms," Clemente came to be labeled a "Neo-Expressionist." The term holds some validity when applied to his New York paintings of 1982–83, which are typified by distortions of form, affinities with "primitive" or tribal arts, and a general feeling of emotional turbulence. But ultimately the label has proven a misnomer, for Clemente's work in recent years has grown increasingly contemplative and meditative, while ranging widely between impulses of pictorialism, abstraction, and the unfettered subconscious.

The ghost of Abstract Expressionism was only one specter that Clemente encountered in New York; the other was the living ghost of Andy Warhol. For any artist of Clemente's generation who came to New York, there was no more influential or pervasive figure in the arts than Warhol, who so effortlessly embodied and reflected the crisis of Western culture. The two met and quickly became friends, although Clemente has often said he never managed to relax in Warhol's presence, due in part to his genuine awe of the elder artist, and in part to his keen awareness of Warhol's withering skepticism of everyone and everything, which he masked with ironic platitudes. In a memoir written for The Museum of Modern Art in 1988 summarizing what he found to be of value in Warhol's work, Clemente touches upon several important themes running through his own:

> *I always thought that the paintings had to do with life and death and grace. I understand the fact that life and death are generalities in contemporary life. Andy Warhol found his subject matter in common places and asked the questions that everybody was too intelligent to ask. He was the exemplary mediator between the meaningful and meaningless, and everything that is simply "vague."*

> *Warhol sought a "democratic" approach to the image, but ideas of liberty and democracy rely on an unlimited space in which to expand. The only unlimited space we have is not the West or the planet but the space of the imagination. Warhol's work is an open-ended list of possible images approached and left behind in total freedom. Is that Modern Art?[6]*

Understandably, those aspects of Warhol's work that Clemente values can also be applied to his own: the search for imagery in "common places," stressing the shared nature of all human experience; the role of the artist as mediator, in the sense of being able both to occupy a middle position between two opposites and to transmit meaning; and the need for every work of art to posit an open-ended set of possibilities that are resistant to any literal or conclusive definitions. This latter category of indeterminacy describes a state in which Warhol lived as well as worked, where his public persona was as much an artistic creation as were the paintings themselves. Clemente recognized this when he said he admired Warhol for his "ritualized . . . presence in the world. I think that is the correct way to live—to live ritually—but that is a gift you get at a certain point in your life if you deserve it."[7]

Figure 43. Andy Warhol, Francesco Clemente, and Jean Michel Basquiat (left to right), New York, September 1984

Figure 44. Jean Michel Basquiat (American, 1960–1988), Francesco Clemente, and Andy Warhol (American, 1928–1987)
Horizontal Painting, 1984
Acrylic, silkscreen, and oil crayon on canvas, 41 x 101″ (104.1 x 256.5 cm)
Courtesy Galerie Bruno Bischofberger, Zurich

Clemente's artistic relationship with Warhol dates to 1984, when, together with Jean Michel Basquiat, the three collaborated on a group of twelve paintings; four paintings were begun by each of the artists, who in turn were given the next group of four to develop, before receiving the final four canvases to complete (Figures 43, 44).[8] The method was similar to the Surrealists' favorite game of the "exquisite corpse," a kind of blind collaboration whereby artists or poets would execute various parts of a drawing or poem without being allowed to see the contributions of the other participants until the work was completed. As intriguing and successful as some of the paintings proved to be, Clemente did not partake in further collaborations along these lines. (Warhol and Basquiat, however, went on to create dozens of paintings together.) In many cases the exercise of dividing the creative act amongst three distinct sensibilities proved more ambiguous than cumulative; the canvases were picked up and delivered to the three artists' studios, so there was no actual contact among them, no opportunity for intuitive exchange. The efforts also brought up Clemente's instinctive feelings of incompatibility with other painters, for as he has often stated, the inspiration for his work derives not from painting but from poetry. Indeed, one of the most rewarding and exhilarating aspects of Clemente's life in New York has proved to be the accessibility of so many of the poets whose literary works paralleled his own conception of picture making. Allen Ginsberg, John Wieners, Robert Creeley, Gregory Corso, and Rene Ricard—all became both friends and collaborators.

For the young Clemente in Naples and Rome, the Beat writers were the living symbols of the true artist: one who delved into the private self in search of a wider definition of man's nature, outside of academism, formalism, or the strictures of society.[9] They were guides for any artist whose innermost fears and joys were the prime area of artistic exploration. Another attraction of the Beat writers lay in their embrace of Eastern thought. Jack Kerouac was raised as a Roman Catholic, and later immersed himself in the philosophy and religions of India, a linking that seemed especially useful to Clemente. A sampling of Kerouac's "List of Essentials,"[10] rules of artistic composition informed by his study of the principles of Buddhist sentience, could serve as a road map for understanding Clemente's work:

> 2. *Submissive to everything, open, listening . . .*
> 5. *Something that you feel will find its own form . . .*
> 8. *Write what you want bottomless from bottom of the mind*
> 9. *The unspeakable visions of the individual . . .*
> 12. *In tranced fixation dreaming upon object before you . . .*
> 16. *The jewel center of interest is the eye within the eye*
> 17. *Write in recollection and amazement for yourself . . .*
> 19. *Accept loss forever*
> 20. *Believe in the holy contour of life*
> 21. *Struggle to sketch the flow that already exists intact in mind*
> 22. *Dont think of words when you stop but to see picture better . . .*
> 24. *No fear or shame in the dignity of yr experience, language & knowledge*

Essentially, Kerouac is insisting upon the nonimposition of "artistic" ideas; for him the calculated work of art will forever be a stillbirth. For the Beat writers, the path of the true artist lies not in imposing a form, but in allowing one to emerge from the thoughts, emotions, and perceptions that inspire. Thus the real point of Clemente's insistence on the need to dispense with hierarchical thinking in art is that we must reject *any* formal ordering of experience that is imposed from without, since such an ordering will inevitably be based upon the lie of intellective reasoning or, even worse, societal values. For the Beats the object of art is illumination, not through exoticism or mysticism, but through the humble recognition of

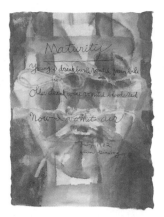

Figure 45. *Maturity*, poem by Allen Ginsberg, 1982,
and illustration by Francesco Clemente, 1985
Watercolor and ink on paper, 26 x 19" (66 x 48.3 cm)
Collection of Herbert and Michelle Rosenfeld, Upper
Saddle River, New Jersey

the holiness of everyday experience. By admitting every aspect of their psyche (however
sordid or trivial) into their work, the Beats conferred upon human experience a dignity
based upon a reverence for *all* of life, and it was for this reason that Kerouac insisted that the
Beat generation was fundamentally a spiritual movement.

Clemente began his collaborations with Allen Ginsberg the day after they met, in March of
1983. Ginsberg visited Clemente in his loft and spent a morning writing out his long poem,
White Shroud (p. 181), completed several weeks previous during his visit to China.[11] This
marked the beginning of a period of collaboration with Ginsberg that continues to this day.
Aside from the great personal warmth and intelligence that Ginsberg emanates, Clemente
responded to the poet's knowledge of William Blake, and his decades of experience with
India and its sacred traditions, which Ginsberg does not approach academically, but as a
means of self-knowledge to be practiced on a daily basis.

Just as Clemente was drawn to the artisans of Jaipur and Orissa as a way of entering into the
traditions of the Indian miniature (see pp. 98–109), his collaborations with Ginsberg are a
means of further exploring the tradition of the illuminated manuscript. These joint projects
combine his two great loves, poetry and painting, in an effort to discover their shared
impulse. From the start, their work together has flowed easefully, as both share a similar
approach to their work based upon meditative practice: passive observation of ordinary
mind; a recognition of illuminative experience; the acceptance of hallucinative or visionary
states of reality; and a willingness to freely explore the erotic impulse and its relation to
creativity.

Once or twice a month Ginsberg would arrive in the mid-morning and sit at a large table in
the artist's studio. There, writing in sketchbooks in pen and ink, he would copy out poems
from typed manuscripts or handwritten notebooks that he had composed during the previous week. Later, after meditating upon the poems in the quiet of his studio, Clemente
would begin painting and decorating the pages, generally with watercolors. Other books
were the result of purely spontaneous collaborations in which poet and painter filled sketchbooks as they sat together. In still other cases, Clemente would provide Ginsberg with
pastel drawings with spaces left empty for texts of the poet's own choosing. The "naked-
ness" of Ginsberg's poetry and his breadth, which ranges from the topical to the transcen-
dental, present Clemente with literal subjects akin to his own. For the poem "Maturity,"
across a sheet of paper a large face is superimposed, the eyes, nose, and mouth tied with
large knots (Figure 45), while the text reads:

> *Young I drank beer & vomited green bile*
> *Older drank wine vomited blood red*
> *Now I vomit air*[12]

In *White Shroud*, Clemente tightly fuses word and image (p. 181); in *Black Shroud*, a corre-
sponding poem, he quietly alters the mood through purely abstract, softly geometric shapes
that create a dirgelike backdrop to Ginsberg's words (p. 183); in *Images from Mind and Space*,
a purely spontaneous collaboration, the verbal and visual elements are of equal import and
weight (p. 180). In each case Clemente's approach varies, and depends entirely on his experience of the poem at the time he sits down with paint and brush; it is his experience of the
poem that is his subject, rather than the poems themselves. In this sense Clemente's contributions are illuminative rather than illustrational. He intercepts the poem at key junctures,
or contributes a pervading image that exists on a distinct yet parallel plane.

Figure 46. Clemente painting a watercolor portrait of John Wieners, New York, 1988

In *Early Morning Exercises* (p. 182),[13] a portfolio of poems by John Wieners (Figure 46), Clemente takes a very different approach to illustrating the text, one that largely derives from Wieners's collagist method of thinking and writing. Educated at Black Mountain College in North Carolina (where he studied with Charles Olson and Robert Creeley), Wieners has lived much of his life as an obscure figure on the fringes of the poetry circles of his native Boston. His work is nearly impossible to define concisely, so vast a range of styles and subjects does it cover. Clemente has often stated that Wieners is his ideal poet, and the affinities between their work are uncanny. A delineation of Wieners's method, written by Allen Ginsberg, might as well be applied to Clemente himself:

> There is a disciplined effort of spontaneity wherein we can read his mind. He leaves evidence of it in the casual conscious breaks in the verse—the urgency to remember what is being thought, capture the flash of enchantment in the mind pictures that pass, leaving words behind, arranged on the page the way they came, as thoughts rose clear enough to indite; so move by move we see his awareness of the line, the helplessness of the line, displayed. Naked line, raw line, vulnerable line, a line of pain so fine it cannot be altered by primping or rougeing (i.e., correcting); his thought already was there, and left its mark.[14]

The texts in *Early Morning Exercises* (ten poems spanning twenty years) reveal an arduous graph of Wieners's emotional life, clothed in fantasy, imagination, guilt, fear, disillusionment, repression, joy, loss, anger, rebellion. His work reveres all that is feminine in nature; it partakes of nostalgia and sentiment but belongs to neither. In numerous poems in the suite Wieners is found ruminating upon the reflection of his face in the mirror, confronting the reality of the discontinuous self. As in "The Face of a Poor Woman," he reassembles the shards of his shattered identity in endless combinations:

> I have the face of a poor woman
> bitter, vindictive
>
> Though somewhat ennobled
> by acts of deprivation from a
>
> man, money, clothes, house.
> All these we had
>
> but taken away by time.
> Now I have only dreams and ambition
>
> to acquire what's given at birth.
> A clear day, steady gait
>
> and mail at the post-office
> plus time to account for my face.[15]

Wieners's love of high camp and transvestism often leads him to write poems in the guise of the opposite sex, unmasking the dominance of gender in language and its latent sexual content. It is a picture of the mind in drag, a means of investing language with an illusory identity that simultaneously deflates that which it exalts.

In illustrating *Early Morning Exercises*, Clemente used an abrupt collage technique, evincing the tenuous nature of Wieners's poems and the opposing forces at work in his mind. After pasting Wieners's manuscript pages onto a portfolio of reproductions of Indian miniatures, Clemente added collaged pages from his Indian notebook of 1976 before decorating the margins in watercolor. To return to a significant notebook of the past is a search for

Figure 47. Francesco Clemente
Silence, from the series *IT*, 1988
Pastel on paper, 26 x 19″ (66 x 48.3 cm)
Courtesy Galerie Bruno Bischofberger, Zurich

Figure 48. Francesco Clemente
Untitled, 1985
Oil on wood, 39¹/₂ x 43¹/₂″ (100.3 x 110.5 cm)
Courtesy Sperone Westwater, New York

Figure 49. Francesco Clemente
Two Boys, 1988
Pigment on linen, 82 x 56″ (208.3 x 142.2 cm)
Courtesy Sperone Westwater, New York

latent meaning, in much the same way that Wieners uncovers hidden meanings in language by disengaging it from conventional or intended usage. It is an acceptance of fragmentation and of the validity of *all* levels of the self.

At their most successful moments, Clemente's excursions into the art of the contemporary illuminated manuscript reveal the ways in which the painter's line and the poet's line are one and the same. It is a search for correspondence, for likemindedness; if not for confirmation, at least for "the company," as Robert Creeley likes to say.

An equivalence of a different but related sort occurs in several publications assembled to document a group of work. Often when assembling exhibition catalogues, Clemente has approached poets to contribute accompanying texts. In so doing he has sought to avoid the banalities of the usual standard critical introduction, and has used the occasion of a publication as a space where word and image can interact. Recent notable books have included *IT* (1989), sixty-four pastels with twelve sonnets by Robert Creeley;[16] *The Gold Paintings* (1990), twelve paintings with a poem by Gregory Corso;[17] and *Sixteen Pastels* (1989), with eleven poems by Rene Ricard.[18]

The sixty-four pastels in *IT* (Figure 47) were drawn in Southampton, New York, in a house by the sea where the artist and his family spent a year following the birth of their twin sons in 1988. It was the most ambitious drawing cycle Clemente had undertaken since "The Pondicherry Pastels" (see pp. 65–68) nearly ten years earlier. Certainly the natural setting of eastern Long Island, with its profusion of wooded areas and flora, induced a softer, more pastoral body of work than what Clemente had been producing in the city proper. It also allowed him the extended period of concentration and continuity needed to pursue such a large series. The subject of the pastels is imaginary flowers, inspired in part by his meditations upon the work of Linnaeus, the eighteenth-century Swedish botanist who ordered the plant kingdom into male and female, and assigned Latin names to each specimen. The pastels are meditations on the world of natural forms, and sexuality and gestation, where vase and flower suggest womb and sexual organs (Figures 48, 49). After completing the series, Clemente sent reproductions of the pastels to Creeley (Figure 50), who then composed pendant poems. Although Creeley was not supplied with a list of titles, in two instances Clemente received poems back that bore the same titles as those that he had assigned to his pastels, a fair indication that the poet and painter were of like minds:

> *I'm a fan of poets, particularly American poets. Creeley's poetry is very pure and his language connects and relates directly to an earlier generation like Cummings and Pound who have great appeal for me. And then what happened with the poems is the idea that finally your things have a voice. I think of all art forms as voice. For me, man's greatest moment must have come before painting, writing, or music, when there was only voice. . . . When two people believe the same thing it becomes a fact. For an artist I don't think there is anything more than that—when another person sees what you see.*[19]

For Creeley, a poem is about the fact of its own writing and not any extrinsic subject. Stated differently, the subject of a poem is the way in which the mind moves within the arbitrary field that is consciousness and the energy that sustains that movement. "For me personally poetry is an intense instant which is either gained or lost in the actual writing," Creeley has said.[20] It is a view of the creative act that is very much akin to Clemente's practice of opening a channel and accepting whatever comes through, denying the controlling impulses of the mind to establish a hierarchy of values, be they formal, emotional, or intellectual. Any close observer of his work will be continually frustrated at his seeming perversity in choosing not to refine a style or repeat a success, but as an artist he is genuinely uninterested in the conse-

Figure 50. Robert Creeley, Naropa Institute, Boulder, Colorado, 1984; photographed by Allen Ginsberg

Figure 51. Gregory Corso, New York, 1988; photographed by Allen Ginsberg

Figure 52. Clemente's New York studio with *The Dark in Me*, from the series *The Gold Paintings*, 1988

quence of his work outside of its actual occurrence. The point, as Creeley has noted, is not to fit experience to possible orders of art or language, but to return art and language to their places *in* experience.[21]

Like his contemporary, the painter Cy Twombly (see Figure 3), the poet Gregory Corso (Figure 51) is an American who has spent much of his adult life in Italy and Greece, finding his inspiration in the Hellenic origins of Western civilization. Throughout his work Corso has delved into the history and myths of ancient Egypt, Greece, and Rome, updating their forms and meters in contemporary vernacular. He retains a devotion to old gods and forgotten oracles, keeping alive in his work the solemn grandeur of antiquity. Clemente had read and revered Corso's work two decades earlier as a youth in Rome, aware that this was a *contemporary* poet fashioning his work out of the classical past. During the summers of 1987 and 1988, the poet was a frequent visitor at Clemente's studio (where they would often sit and watch Italian soccer matches on television).

In December of 1988, Corso visited Clemente in his studio and saw a group of recently completed paintings in terra-cotta and black pigments on gold-leafed canvas, with each work marked by a conspicuous pair of eyes (Figure 52). Weird and anomalous even for an *oeuvre* such as Clemente's, these primeval-like paintings seemed utterly unrelated to any previous work. For over a week Corso visited and revisited the studio, filling a notebook with lines and couplets, studying the paintings, digging at their meaning. (Eventually Clemente asked Corso to title the works as well, feeling now fully outside of them.) As a poet who thinks in archetypes, Corso recognized the Etruscan affinities in Clemente's *Gold Paintings*, and responded with a long poem on the theme of origins and the cyclical nature of life in all forms: cosmic, mythic, historical, biological. "Go back to your sources, I tell people," Corso once replied when asked his advice to young poets, ". . . and this I might have gotten from the Tibetans, because they say if you're conscious on your death bed, try to think back to your mother's cunt because you came in as you go out. It's good exercise for poets. I had to go back through history to get back as far as I could go to the sources, cave paintings as I say, and all that."[22]

Eventually, in the published book, *The Gold Paintings*, Clemente created a sequence between paintings and poems, interspersed with impressionistic photographs by Adam Füss. God, earth, fire, clay, ice, darkness—Corso's imagery speaks of a primeval, elemental world, one that echoes Clemente's pictographic outlines of teeth, antlers, hand prints, and burial mounds. The earth, both tomb and womb, opens in triangular crevices. In fact these paintings had their inadvertent origins in a rock-crystal yoni that Clemente had acquired and placed on a table in the center of his studio. It is the inescapable presence of this sculpture— the Hindu icon for Shakti, represented in the shape of a vulva—that pervades these works.

Clemente's fraternity with the poet Rene Ricard (Figure 53) extends back to the painter's first visit to New York, when Ricard was then at the height of his reign of terror over high society and the New York art world. Poet, critic, movie star, wit, Ricard has been a singular presence in New York for twenty-five years. He appeared in many of Andy Warhol's underground film classics (including the notorious *Chelsea Girls*) as the essence of cruel and beautiful youth, much loved for his warmth and humor, and much feared for his devastating wit.

Although he seldom read or published his works, Ricard's reputation as a poet steadily grew during the 1970s. His poems speak of the urban experience, ironic and deprecating, always with a slight twist; their paradoxical blend of lyricism and mannerism seems to sum up much of the spirit of our age. His epigrams, brutally stark, recall those of the great Latin poet Catullus in their exploration of the common root of love and hate. Like his fellow Bos-

Figure 53. Rene Ricard, New York, 1987; photographed by Allen Ginsberg

tonian John Wieners (of whom Ricard was a youthful protégé), his work is a product of both great style and utter artlessness. In an unpublished text about the poet, Clemente summed up Ricard's uncompromising personality:

> *He is not possessed by a tragic destiny, only an exceptional objectivity. He has never owned a book, and if he speaks of things he has read it is as if he heard them from a voice—but whose and when and where? Hungry & exhausted, he asks for a $300 loan, only to return with a $350 bouquet, obtained at a discount. While posing for a portrait he disappears. Two days later I find him asleep behind a pile of canvas. We are left with nothing except our own body, and our mystery is to be what we are. He achieves maturity who expresses himself justly, in the right place at the right time—and therefore is believed a poet when merely absorbed timidly in the contemplation of the gnarls of a chimerical and moral weave. Constructing elegant theories through his love for the word that wounds. Wounded by poetry, we take refuge in a shelter that lies scorched in the wake that Rene leaves behind.*[23]

When the cultural history of New York in our time is written, Rene Ricard must occupy a position of great importance. The essence of his work lies in the utter abandon with which it is created, for despite the many excesses of his personality, as a poet Ricard stands alone in his generation for his insistence upon the inspired moment as the rightful domain of all art.

Given his temperament, it is doubtful that anyone could actively collaborate with Ricard. *Sixteen Pastels* is more properly a convergence in time and place of two analogous sensibilities. Clemente had prepared the publication to accompany a London exhibition, but was unsuccessful at finding a complementary text. On the day he was sending the book to press, Ricard appeared at his studio and deposited a tiny handmade manuscript book for safekeeping. Its subjects were, in the poet's words, "Love, death, and trying to find an apartment in New York."[24] Recognizing the synergy between Ricard's poems and his own images, Clemente merely appended a facsimile of Ricard's manuscript book as an afterword to the pastels. In this case, the collaboration was simply a matter of the two artists sharing the same space as kindred spirits.

The emotional fragility of Ricard's poems was only heightened by the faint typewriting on the translucent vellum manuscript book, which he had sewn together with pink thread. An intensely *visual* poet with a wide knowledge of the history of art, Ricard's work often seems to blur the distinction between the visual and verbal, as in the poem "*SPRING FOG, NINTH FLOOR*" from *Sixteen Pastels*:

> *DAWN*
> *A WHITE CAT*
> *CLAWS THE SKYSCRAPERS*
> *IT WOULD APPEAR*
> *WHO EVER DESIGNED THE*
> *HOLOGRAM POSING AS THE VIEW*
> *FROM MY (FAKE?) WINDOW*
> *FLUNKED ELEMENTARY PERSPECTIVE*
> *AND GEOGRAPHY*
> *ADDING EXTRA AVENUES*
> *TOWARDS THE WEST*
>
> *WHEN A PAINTER CAN'T THINK UP*
> *A PICTURE*
> *THEY WRITE*
> *I PAINTED THIS*[25]

If there is a single element shared by all of the poets with whom Clemente has collaborated, it is their common fealty to the work of Ezra Pound. Although Clemente has often stated his abhorrence of many of Pound's political ideas, as a literary figure the American expatriate poet occupies a central place in Clemente's aesthetics.

Ezra Pound stands as the foremost example of an artist exploring a multicultural, non-hierarchical view of civilization. In *The Cantos*, his magnum opus of human consciousness, he rejects the nineteenth-century positivist view of history as a time line in which people, places, and things are parceled out into neatly separate units. Pound replaces this order with an open form, a space-time continuum extending simultaneously forward and backward. History is seen as a product of human consciousness no different from the disciplines of mythology, literature, or religion. All are shifting conceptions of the mortal mind. For Pound these conceptions are rooted solely in the emotions and imagination of man, and are, moreover, continually in flux. Thus it seems natural to Pound that the manufactured images of the artistic imagination should possess the same objective reality as any other object or idea in this world of forms.

Throughout *The Cantos*, Pound continually draws what he calls "subject-rhymes"—families of forms or ideas that recur through the ages. Orpheus becomes Dionysus who in turn becomes Christ; Venus is united with Gilgamesh and Shiva. In the words of one writer, "Pound has found a form that can weave the lyrical, the factual and the didactic into a single texture."[26] Pound restores the ancient gods and mysteries by demonstrating that they are still with us, only in slightly different forms. For Clemente, Pound represents the quintessential artist of our age, one who with exquisite clarity and skill has created a system capable of admitting all forms, styles, or subjects in his search for common values.

Pound's method for compressing space and fusing disparate elements in the poem is the concept of the ideogram, a kind of word-picture. "An 'Image' is that which presents an intellectual and emotional complex in an instant of time,"[27] Pound once wrote. It is a definition derived in large part from his reading of Ernest Fenollosa's *The Chinese Written Character as a Medium for Poetry*.[28] Fenollosa notes that the Chinese character for *red* contains pictographic references to blood, rust, the setting sun, and numerous other physical manifestations of the concept of redness. Thus each ideogram exists as a tiny nexus of vivid images wherein, Clemente has noted, "each element of the language is a link in a chain of meaning, ever changing and ever shifting. You can never see one of these elements by itself, but only in a chain of meaning and not for what it is but what it reminds you of: what it is not."[29] A prime appeal of the ideogram is its ability to short-circuit the rational mind. It possesses a unity that the alphabetical word-unit can never have, since ideas can be demonstrated rather than merely referred to.

For Clemente, as for Pound before him, the ideogrammatic method satisfies that ancient occult yearning to relate everything to everything else as evidence of an original unity. Yet as a concept it is also closer to the actual dynamic of perception and the ways in which images are generated by the mind, not in isolation but in analogous clusters of subject or form. The combination of disparate or even unrelated images to yield a third image that contains a new meaning (quite apart from the individual meaning of the two elements being combined) lay at the foundation of Pound's thinking. The implications of this idea for Clemente are vast, as can be seen in the several thousand drawings that he produced in the decade of the 1970s and the paintings that issued from them in the 1980s. It means that instead of painting from any preconceived idea or as a method of depiction, one might seek to uncover a part of one's self in the act of drawing, of creating an image for the purpose of seeing what it might look like; it becomes a way of discovering what one did not know.

Thus it is the ideogrammatic concept of the poetic image that lies at the heart of Clemente's works on paper, for in many respects his drawings function as ideograms in themselves: taut, highly charged images, emblematic, midway between symbol and allegory. There is one crucial difference in Clemente's case, and that is that no etymology can be traced, for these are invented ideograms based on imaginary laws: they cannot be decoded because there is no code, or if one existed, it was consumed in the making:

> *The images are results not of a focus, of focusing on a good idea, but of wandering from one idea to another without giving more weight to one or the other. . . . Since the work is an image, you can't tell where it began, and you forget where you began. So what you see there, I don't know myself. I made a safe; I invented the safe, and I lost the key. And losing the key makes the work, gives the work this autonomy. It cannot be reduced. It cannot be brought back to its original elements. That makes it objectively poetical.*[30]

An irreducible element—capable of being apprehended in its entirety yet incapable of being brought into a simpler state—the image functions as a mediation between the visible world of forms and perceptions, and the invisible world of thoughts and emotions. For Clemente the creation of an image is the result of centering one's attention or activity upon a single point, not unlike the discipline of yoga or meditation. It is a visual synthesis of diverse and complex elements that form an hermetic system, impervious to theory or logic, yet open to multiple definitions. And by its indivisibility the image possesses a oneness that in centuries past was the province of divinity.

Interestingly, it was exactly when Clemente had at last achieved a much desired distance from Italy that he returned to the subject of his homeland in a work that proved a vast summation of so many of his themes and motives. These were the illustrations for Alberto Savinio's *The Departure of the Argonaut*,[31] a book that Clemente has called "a collaboration between an Italian and a foreigner. I am the foreigner."[32]

In 1983 Clemente was approached by Petersburg Press in New York to create a work in the deluxe tradition of the *livre d'artiste*. The text he chose to illustrate was Savinio's *The Departure of the Argonaut*, a kaleidoscopic account of the author's experiences fighting for his homeland in the First World War. In selecting a text that was written at the outset of the modernist movement, Clemente was intentionally overstepping a previous generation to forge a link with that of his grandfather, as if searching for the thread that had been broken by the years of fascist domination.

Clemente's edition of *The Departure of the Argonaut* (p. 178) stands as one of the half-dozen finest illustrated books in the twentieth century. Working in intense, intermittent spells for approximately three years, Clemente countered Savinio's capriciousness with a visual suppleness that inspires every page. It is perhaps the only individual work of Clemente's *oeuvre* from which one may reconstruct the themes and subjects that had been recurring up until that time. For Clemente, Savinio's *Argonaut* is suffused with a sense of longing for the loss of Italy as "a civilized place, in the sense of a place of lightness, of femininity and refinement."[33] His own illustrations to *The Departure of the Argonaut* are an homage to an aspect of Italy that the artist feels has been sadly lost.

Savinio is very much a writer in the picaresque tradition of European literature that Clemente so keenly admires, which includes Laurence Sterne, Jonathan Swift, and Thomas de Quincey. All are authors whose works are dominated by their sensibility; they do not adhere to any one literary convention but create their own forms, elastic enough to contain the many extravagances of their personalities. Fancy, artifice, imagination, contradiction, virtuosity, licentiousness—all are present in abundance, yet always with the requisite *lightness* of touch.

Despite his ingenious originality, Savinio is essentially a classical author whose work recalls the episodic narrations of Apuleius, Petronius, and Boccaccio. The author explores the concept of the antique with a broad array of tools, some of which he can rightfully claim to have invented: literary digressions and allusions, linguistic puns, dreams, occult symbols, popular songs, advertising slogans, mythology, and a babel of languages that includes English, French, German, Spanish, Latin, Greek, Turkish, Amharic, Ladino, and Esperanto. Eventually, Savinio's discursions fully obscure the narrative. It is impossible to experience the text passively; readers must allow themselves to become totally engaged in the writing, or they are utterly excluded.

"*The Departure of the Argonaut* is a text which is continually opening, unfolding, elaborating—but never explaining," Clemente has remarked.[34] Pursuing this impulse the artist presents his images in a similarly open-ended manner. The literary content of each page is distilled into an emblem. There is a tripartite ordering of time frames: Clemente is working in a contemporary mode while looking back at the origins of modernism in Savinio's writing, who is in turn looking back at antiquity.

The Departure of the Argonaut is an attempt to reconcile a classical heritage with contemporary vision. As Savinio wanders in the novel through the semi-Greek cities of southern Italy, the pagan flavor of late antiquity persists. His world exists in a confluence where cultures disintegrate, one into the next. This is the resonant past, which charges the present. Savinio views the concept of civilization as a vast tomb, with the dead to be both revered and looted. (For the classical artist borrowing was no crime.) The accumulations of the past had indeed already reached overwhelming proportions by late antiquity, when the Roman emperor Julian the Apostate admonished the cult of saints: "You keep adding the corpses newly dead to the corpses of long ago. You have filled the whole world with tombs and sepulchers."[35] An identical complaint might be lodged today against the canon of art.

In this labyrinth of rumination, Savinio continually taxes the reader's comprehension through the cultivation of facts and references that have no practical application. Thus intellectual delectation takes supremacy over all other activities, through that uniquely Italian wedding of intellect with pleasure. Both text and image are examples of quintessential dilettantism in the uncorrupted sense of the word, which derives from the Latin verb *dilectare*: "to delight in." The mordant wit of author and artist occupy opposite sides of the same coin, which might be described as an overly effusive imagination held in check by a highly developed sense of drollery.

In his illustrations to *The Departure of the Argonaut*, Clemente relies upon a wide range of sources. Images are drawn from life (his face in a mirror), from memory (the Adriatic coast), from books (Italian locomotives circa 1915), from engineering blueprints (the mechanical rendering of a battleship), from technical manuals (the nautical flags that spell *Savinio* in semaphore), and from photographs of botanical specimens. In some cases the natural imperfections or fossils in the lithographic stone would prompt an image. In another instance, Clemente discovered a stone that still bore a nineteenth-century cartographer's rendering of mountainous terrain, which he accepted as an *objet trouvé*, wittily turning the image on its side and altering the mountains with a brush until they read as ocean waves, an image directly inspired by Savinio's metaphor of the sea as solid rock. For each page of the book Clemente forced himself to come up with not merely new images, but new ways of *seeing* images in the world around him.

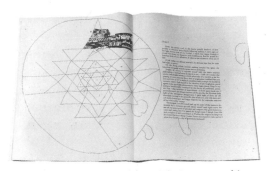

Figure 54. Opening spread from *The Departure of the Argonaut*; Italian text by Alberto Savinio, 1917 (English translation by George Scrivani, 1986), and lithographs by Francesco Clemente, 1983, 1985, 1986
Book of bound letterpress and lithographs on mold-made Okawara kozo paper; 25¾ x 20″ (65.4 x 50.8 cm) (sheet)
Published by Petersburg Press, New York, 1986
Collection of Raymond Foye, New York

On the first page of the *Argonaut*, Clemente has inscribed the great Hindu mandala, the schematized figuration of the cosmos (Figure 54). Nestled within one of the segments of the mandala—each of which, in mythology, is controlled by a separate deity—is a delicate rendering of a Roman ruin. Clemente's *mise en page* is impeccable, and the image has a sense of rightness to it, as if to remind us that all gods are one. It is an expression of interchangeability, or better, interconnectiveness. (In Jungian terms the mandala is the symbol of the perpetual effort to reunify the self.) At the bottom of the page, in outline, are Roman fasciae, phallic emblems. This is the game of the sacred and the profane. On the second page of the book we are confronted by a flat printing of transparent white in the exact position of the mandala, conveying the equally legitimate (and even necessary) possibility of total absence of image.

As Clemente settled into a new life in New York he soon began traveling throughout the United States, driving across the southern and western states, and spending considerable time living and working in the Southwest. One of the dominant qualities about America that impressed Clemente and gradually found its way into his work was the vast sense of open space. As his sense of the spirit of the land and knowledge of the indigenous American tribes grew, his conception of the country as merely an extension of Europe fell away: "I discovered America when I came [to America]," Clemente later recalled. "Seen from Europe, people think of America as a sort of intensified Europe, where all the things you don't like about Europe are at their utmost intensity. It seems that in Europe, people can't come to terms with the idea that America has nothing to do with Europe. . . . Having spent time in India, I realize that America is farther away from Europe than India is."[36]

The exhilaration Clemente derived from immersing himself in the sheer enormity of the physical space of the North American continent became another means of testing and abstracting his own creative responses and impulses, of locating within himself the contours and boundaries of a specific place. In the case of the Southwest, it was a diaphanous quality that impressed him, a feeling of "thinness" or "lightness," as he described it: "I . . . walked around in the desert and saw this very slight makeup the American Indians left on the desert, just this thin layer of graffiti and broken pots . . . . Where a village had been you see a slight curve; they just lightly curved the piazza around which they lived. . . . In India or in Europe, you have foundations that go miles down into the earth. But here it seems that civilization has always, for thousands and thousands of years, been a matter of a very light film."[37]

It is this quality of lightness—or delicacy, luminosity, or weightlessness, however one might characterize it—that increasingly emerges in Clemente's work in the 1980s. Unfortunately it is a quality that eludes most critics, as the underground film maker Jack Smith, an early influence on the young Clemente in Rome, wryly notes: "I know absolutely that we do not know the names of our really great films. All we know about is the heaviest stuff the critics went for, because all they can recognize is the quality of heaviness. Lightness doesn't register on them, and yet lightness is one of the true eternal qualities that art essentially must possess. It isn't heaviness."[38] *Lightness* is one of Clemente's favorite words, and his main strategy for getting out from under the weight of tradition, formalism, ideology—all of the accepted and received suppositions with which we are burdened. And, as Clemente has repeatedly said, it is only through a constant denial of the accepted hierarchies in life as well as art that we might step outside of the straitjacket of what we know.

As Clemente has wandered throughout this world, seeking a common place in the diversity of life, he has not so much imposed a form as allowed one to emerge. In the body of the world the same force that rules the stars and seas rules our lives, and the works in this catalogue speak to that process. Accepting his own creativity as the only possible form of unity, these works constitute fragments of a greater whole, one that is still becoming visible. All of the facts of our existence are here, without heroism or idealism. In an increasingly despiritualized world, Clemente's meditations reanimate existence itself through the renewal of vision and therefore the constant renewal of the mind. Like Pound's great graph of consciousness, *The Cantos*, Clemente's visual meanderings comprise a cosmology, an organic and open-ended system, complete unto itself and capable of embodying all of the elements of the physical and psychic world. His work is intensely about lived experience, where memory, imagination, intuition, and emotion are linked in an expression of the ineffable mysteries that continue to unite the ancient world with the modern.

1. Charles Olson, *Human Universe and Other Essays*, ed. Donald Allen (New York, 1967), p. 10.

2. Quoted in Robin White, "Francesco Clemente," *View*, vol. 3, no. 6 (November 1981), p. 2.

3. "Manners Entice: A Discussion Between Alex Katz and Francesco Clemente," *Parkett*, no. 21 (September 1989), p. 50.

4. Whitechapel Art Gallery, London, *Francesco Clemente: The Fourteen Stations* (January 7–February 20, 1983).

5. Stedelijk Museum, Amsterdam, *Willem de Kooning: Nordatlantens ljus/The North Atlantic Light 1960–1983* (May 11–July 3, 1983). Also shown at the Louisiana Museum of Modern Art, Humlebaek (July 15–September 4, 1983); and the Moderna Museet, Stockholm (September 17–October 30, 1983), which is where Clemente saw the exhibition.

6. Manuscript as submitted to The Museum of Modern Art, New York.

7. Francesco Clemente, interview with Lisa Phillips, March 27, 1989. The interview was conducted in English and all quotes are taken from this transcript. An edited version of the interview appeared in *Beaux Arts Magazine*, no. 69 (June 1989), pp. 91–95, 159–60, under the title "Exposition Clemente: Les chemins de la sagesse," and included a summary in English.

8. See also Galerie Bruno Bischofberger, Zurich, *Collaborations: Jean-Michel Basquiat, Francesco Clemente, Andy Warhol* (September 15–October 13, 1984).

9. A concise definition of the Beat generation is offered by one of its participants, the novelist John Clellon Holmes: "The Beat attitude, to call it that, was protesting against what we felt was an inadequate conception of the nature of man." Holmes remarks further: "If you accept the modern world on its terms, and are content with it, then anyone who can't function in it is strange, bent, twisted, etc., but one of the qualities in the Beat movement was the recognition that madness was a kind of retreat for those who wanted to stay privately sane. We understood that madness meant pain, as any withdrawal does, but the idea that there was any way to formulate social sanity was one of the things we tried to give up, just as we tried to give up Freudianism, Marxism, and all determinisms." From "An Interview with John Clellon Holmes, by John Tytell," in Arthur Knight and Kit Knight, eds., *Kerouac and the Beats: A Primary Sourcebook* (New York, 1988), p. 163.

The writers of the Beat generation had the good fortune of being translated into Italian by Fernanda Pivano, perhaps the finest English-Italian translator of her generation. Having established her reputation as the translator of Ernest Hemingway, F. Scott Fitzgerald, Gertrude Stein, and others, she soon turned to translating the Beat writers shortly after they began publishing in their own country, thus affording them prestige abroad that is still withheld them at home. Consequently, when Clemente came to New York, he arrived with a wide knowledge of and appreciation for the Beats.

10. Jack Kerouac, *Heaven & Other Poems* (San Francisco, 1977), p. 47.

11. Allen Ginsberg, *White Shroud: Poems 1980–1985* (New York, 1986), pp. 47–50.

12. Ibid., p. 30.

13. The title *Early Morning Exercises* was provided by Wieners, after spending the better part of one morning in Boston carefully copying a selection of his poems for Clemente to illustrate. (The title is also an oblique reference to yogic exercises.)

14. Allen Ginsberg, "Foreword," in John Wieners, *Selected Poems: 1958–1984*, ed. Raymond Foye (Santa Barbara, 1986), p. 15.

15. Wieners, *Poems*, p. 250.

16. Francesco Clemente and Robert Creeley, *IT* (Zurich: Bruno Bischofberger Edition, 1989).

17. Francesco Clemente and Gregory Corso, *The Gold Paintings* (Zurich: Bruno Bischofberger Edition, 1990).

18. Francesco Clemente and Rene Ricard, *Sixteen Pastels* (London: Anthony d'Offay Gallery, 1989).

19. Clemente, interview with Phillips.

20. Robert Creeley, interview with Raymond Foye, 1989.

21. Robert Creeley, *The Collected Essays of Robert Creeley* (Berkeley, 1989), p. 124.

22. Gregory Corso, "Interview with Robert King," in Arthur Knight and Kit Knight, eds., *The Beat Vision: A Primary Sourcebook* (New York, 1987), p. 153.

23. Francesco Clemente, "Aiming at Rene," 1990 (unpublished manuscript).

24. Rene Ricard, interview with Raymond Foye, May 1989. For further Ricard publications see *Rene Ricard, 1979–1980* (New York, 1979); *God with Revolver, Poems 1979–82* (Madras and New York, 1989); and *Trusty Sarcophagus Co.* (New York and Rome, 1990).

25. Clemente and Ricard, *Sixteen Pastels*, n.p.

26. William Cookson, "Some Notes on *Rock-Drill* and *Thrones*," in "Special Issue in Honor of Ezra Pound's Eightieth Birthday," *Agenda*, vol. 4, no. 2 (October–November 1965), pp. 30–37.

27. Ezra Pound, "A Retrospect," in Ezra Pound, *Literary Essays of Ezra Pound*, ed. T. S. Eliot (New York, 1968), p. 4.

28. Ernest Fenollosa, *The Chinese Written Character as a Medium for Poetry*, ed. Ezra Pound (San Francisco, 1964). For a discussion of Oriental ideography and modern poetry, see Laszlo K. Géfin, *Ideogram: History of a Poetic Method* (Austin, 1982). For a specific discussion of Pound and Fenollosa, see Achilles Fang, "Fenollosa and Pound," *Harvard Journal of Asian Studies*, vol. 20 (1957), pp. 213–38.

29. Rainer Crone and Georgia Marsh, *Clemente: An Interview with Francesco Clemente* (New York, 1987), p. 42.

30. Ibid., pp. 42–43.

31. Alberto Savinio, *The Departure of the Argonaut*, with illustrations by Francesco Clemente (New York: Petersburg Press, 1986). Reprinted in a reduced facsimile on the occasion of the exhibition of *The Departure of the Argonaut*, organized by The Museum of Modern Art, New York (December 11, 1986–February 10, 1987).

32. Interview with Rainer Crone and Georgia Marsh, May 1986; this quote is taken from the unedited transcripts that were later published in Crone and Marsh, *Clemente*.

33. Ibid.

34. Francesco Clemente, interview with Raymond Foye, June 1986.

35. Julian the Apostate, Contra Galileo, 335C; quoted in Peter Brown, *The Cult of Saints* (Chicago, 1981), p.7.

36. Crone and Marsh, *Clemente*, p. 39.

37. Ibid.

38. Jack Smith, *Historical Treasures*, ed. Ira Cohen (Madras and New York: Hanuman Books, 1990), pp. 128–29.

Tondo, 1981
Soft-ground etching and aquatint on handmade paper
diameter 16¹/₂″ (41.9 cm) (sheet), 14¹/₂″
(36.8 cm) (plate)
Trial proof; edition of 25; printed by Hidekatsu
Takada and Peter Pettengill, Oakland;
published by Crown Point Press, San Francisco
Crown Point Press, San Francisco and New York

Telamon No. 1, 1981
Etching, aquatint, drypoint, soft-ground
etching, and *chine collé* on handmade paper
62¾ x 24½" (159.4 x 62.2 cm) (sheet),
61 x 19" (154.9 x 48.3 cm) (plate)
Edition 9/25; printed by Hidekatsu Takada and
Peter Pettengill, Oakland; published by Crown
Point Press, San Francisco
Philadelphia Museum of Art. Purchased:
SmithKline Beckman Corporation Fund.
1982-80-2

Telamon No. 2, 1981
Etching, aquatint, drypoint, soft-ground
etching, and *chine collé* on handmade paper
63 x 24½" (160 x 62.2 cm) (sheet), 61 x 19"
(154.9 x 48.3 cm) (plate)
Trial proof; edition of 25; printed by Hidekatsu
Takada and Peter Pettengill, Oakland;
published by Crown Point Press, San Francisco
Crown Point Press, San Francisco
and New York

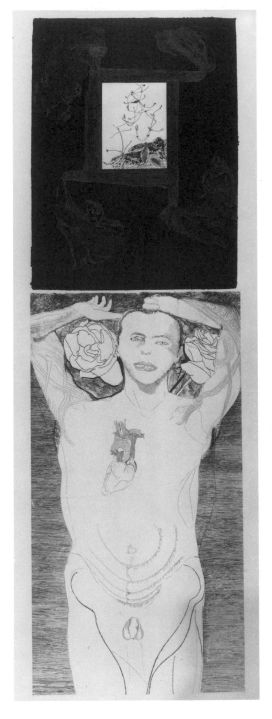

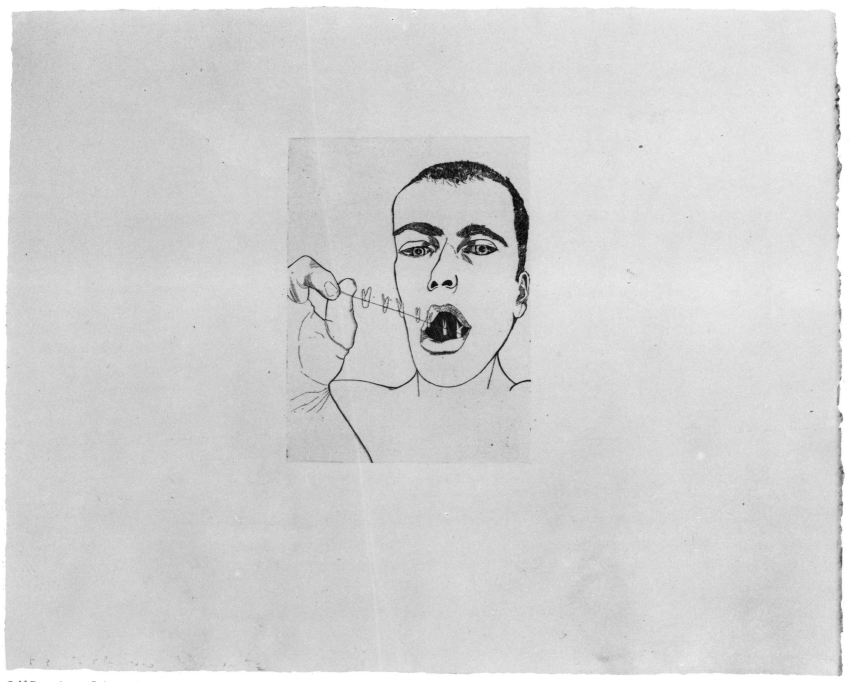

Self-Portrait as a Saint, 1981
Etching on Arches Satine paper
16¹/₈ x 20¹/₄″ (41 x 51.4 cm) (sheet), 7⁷/₈ x 5⁷/₈″
(20 x 14.9 cm) (plate)
Artist's proof; edition of 10 and 10 artist's
proofs; printed by Hidekatsu Takada and Peter
Pettengill, Oakland; published by Crown Point
Press, San Francisco
Philadelphia Museum of Art. Purchased:
SmithKline Beckman Corporation Fund.
1982-80-1

The Twins, 1982
Spitbite on Somerset paper
30 x 44″ (76.2 x 111.8 cm) (sheet), 24 x 36″
(61 x 91.4 cm) (plate)
Artist's proof 5; edition of 15 and 11 artist's
proofs; printed by Hidekatsu Takada and Peter
Pettengill, Oakland; published by Crown Point
Press, San Francisco
Crown Point Press, San Francisco
and New York

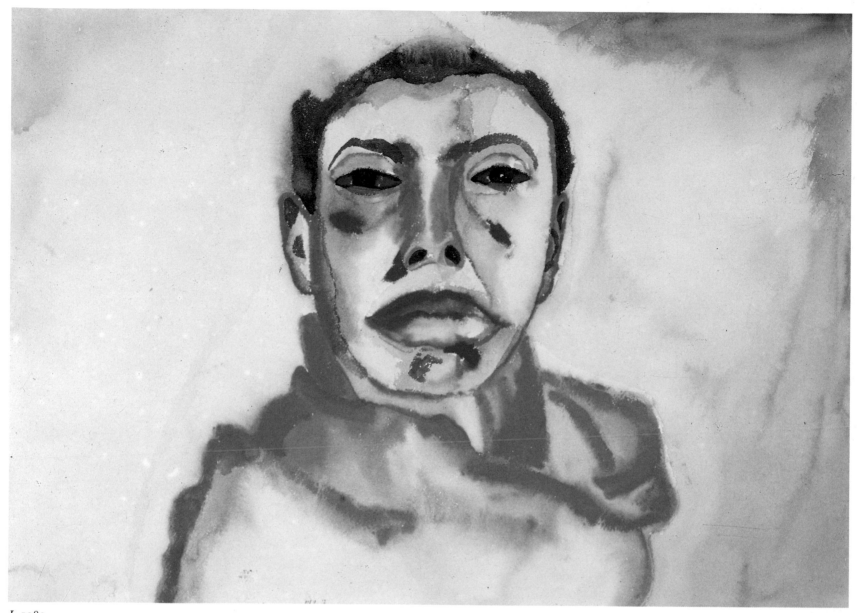

I, 1982
Watercolor on Arches paper
14¹/₁₆ x 20″ (35.7 x 50.8 cm)
Courtesy Thomas Ammann, Zurich

Morning, 1982
Watercolor on Arches paper
14¹/₁₆ x 20″ (35.7 x 50.8 cm)
Courtesy Thomas Ammann, Zurich

Fire, 1982
Watercolor on Arches paper
14¹/₁₆ x 20″ (35.7 x 50.8 cm)
Courtesy Thomas Ammann, Zurich

Books, 1982
Watercolor on Arches paper
14¹/₁₆ x 20″ (35.7 x 50.8 cm)
Courtesy Thomas Ammann, Zurich

Smoke in the Room, 1982
Watercolor on Arches paper
14¹/₁₆ x 20″ (35.7 x 50.8 cm)
Courtesy Thomas Ammann, Zurich

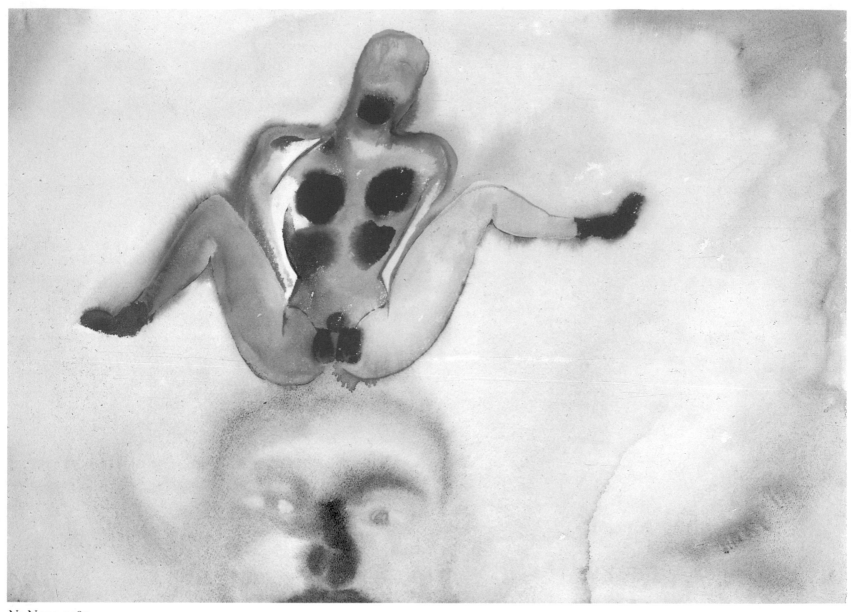

No Name, 1982
Watercolor on Arches paper
14¹/₁₆ x 20″ (35.7 x 50.8 cm)
Courtesy Thomas Ammann, Zurich

Alba and Francesco, 1982
Watercolor on Arches paper
14¹⁄₁₆ x 20″ (35.7 x 50.8 cm)
Courtesy Thomas Ammann, Zurich

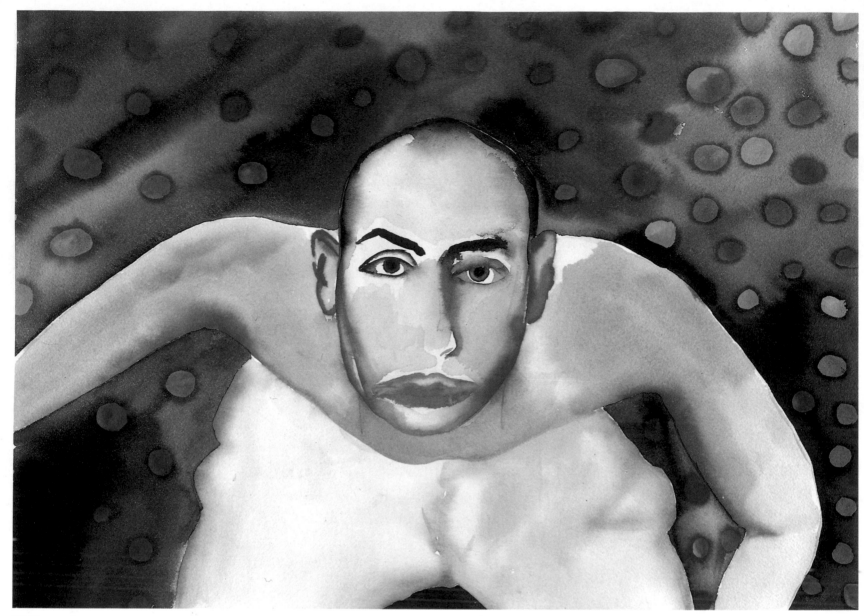

Waiting, 1982
Watercolor on Arches paper
14¹/₁₆ x 20″ (35.7 x 50.8 cm)
Courtesy Thomas Ammann, Zurich

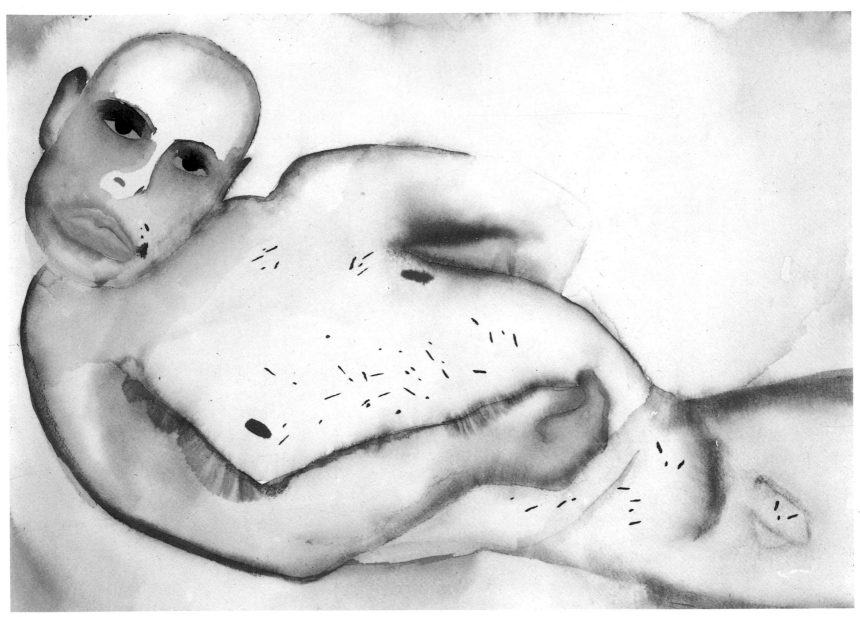

Skin, 1982
Watercolor on Arches paper
14 1/16 x 20" (35.7 x 50.8 cm)
Courtesy Thomas Ammann, Zurich

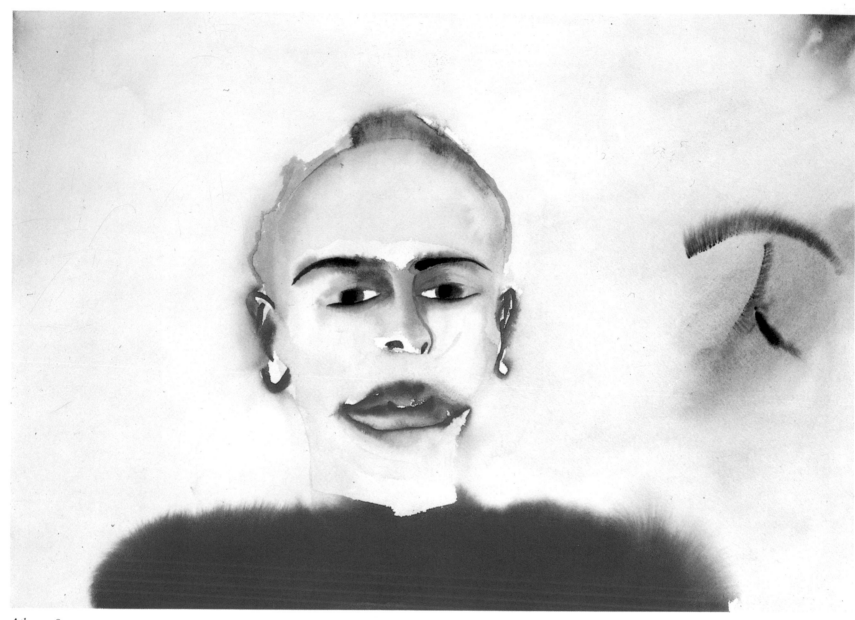

Atlas, 1982
Watercolor on Arches paper
14¹/₁₆ x 20″ (35.7 x 50.8 cm)
Courtesy Thomas Ammann, Zurich

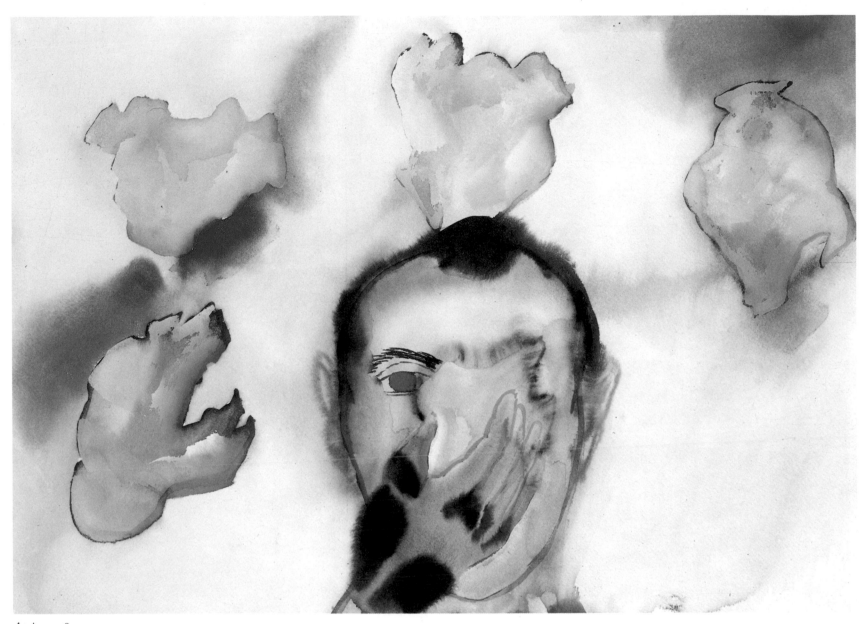

Amico, 1982
Watercolor on Arches paper
14¹/₁₆ x 20″ (35.7 x 50.8 cm)
Courtesy Thomas Ammann, Zurich

Self-Portrait, 1981
Gouache on Arches paper
14¹⁄₁₆ x 20″ (35.7 x 50.8 cm)
Courtesy Thomas Ammann, Zurich

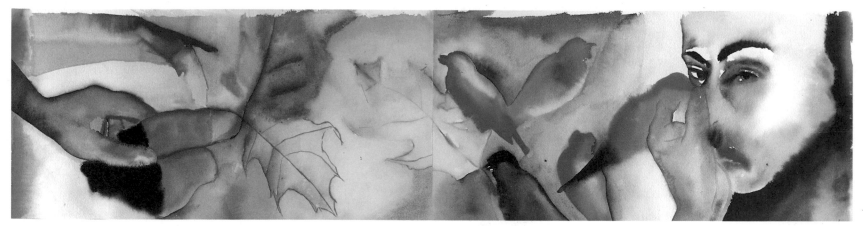

The Future of the Nose, 1983
Watercolor on paper
10¹/₄ x 36¹/₂" (26 x 92.7 cm)
Courtesy Thomas Ammann, Zurich

Solitude, 1982
Four-panel folding screen, watercolor on paper
each panel 72 x 24″ (182.9 x 61 cm)
Courtesy Thomas Ammann, Zurich

She and She, 1982
Pastel on Rives paper
24 x 18″ (61 x 45.8 cm)
Courtesy Thomas Ammann, Zurich

Air, from the series
"The Four Elements," 1982
Pastel on Rives paper
24 x 18″ (61 x 45.8 cm)
Collection of Helen N. Lewis and Marvin B.
Meyer, Beverly Hills, California

Water, from the series
"The Four Elements," 1982
Pastel on Rives paper
24 x 18″ (61 x 45.8 cm)
Private Collection

Fire, from the series
"The Four Elements," 1982
Pastel on Rives paper
24 x 18″ (61 x 45.8 cm)
Collection of Ronald Krueck, Chicago

Earth, from the series
"The Four Elements," 1982
Pastel on Rives paper
24 x 18″ (61 x 45.8 cm)
PaineWebber Group Inc., New York

Yellow, from the series
"The Four Elements," 1982
Pastel on Rives paper
24 x 18″ (61 x 45.8 cm)
Private Collection

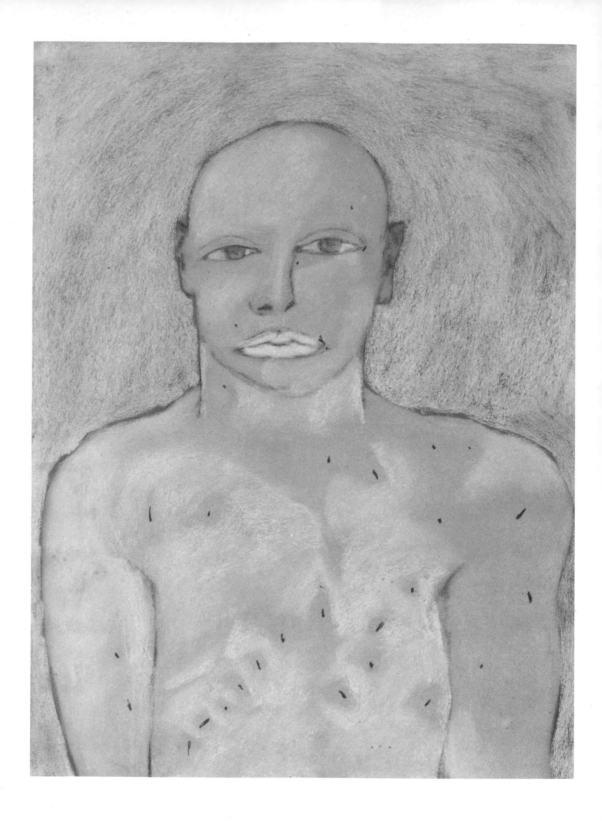

Non ti ricordo, 1982
Pastel on Rives paper
24 x 18″ (61 x 45.8 cm)
Private Collection, Courtesy Galerie Bruno
Bischofberger, Zurich

Furniture, 1983
Pastel on Rives paper
26 x 19″ (66 x 48.2 cm)
Private Collection, Courtesy Galerie Bruno
Bischofberger, Zurich

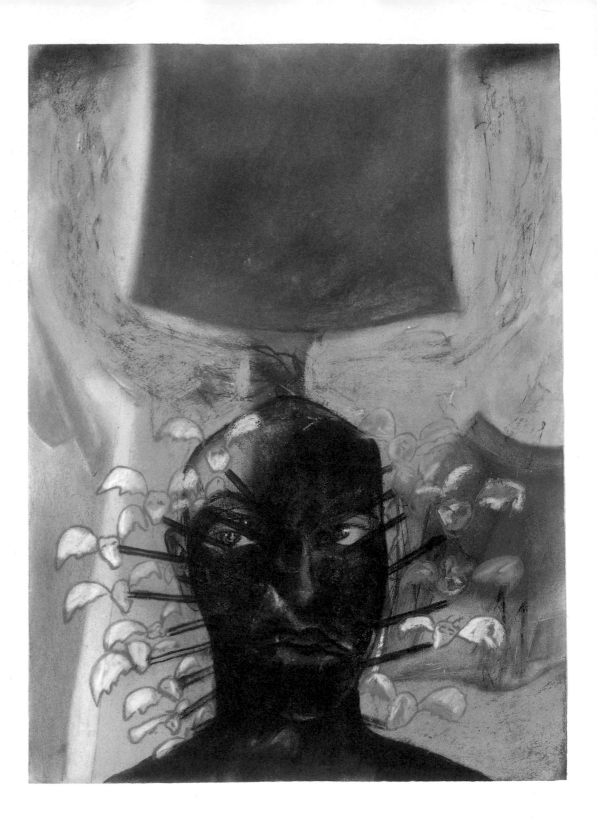

Smoke in the Room, 1983
Pastel on Rives paper
26 x 19" (66 x 48.2 cm)
Private Collection, Courtesy Galerie Bruno
Bischofberger, Zurich

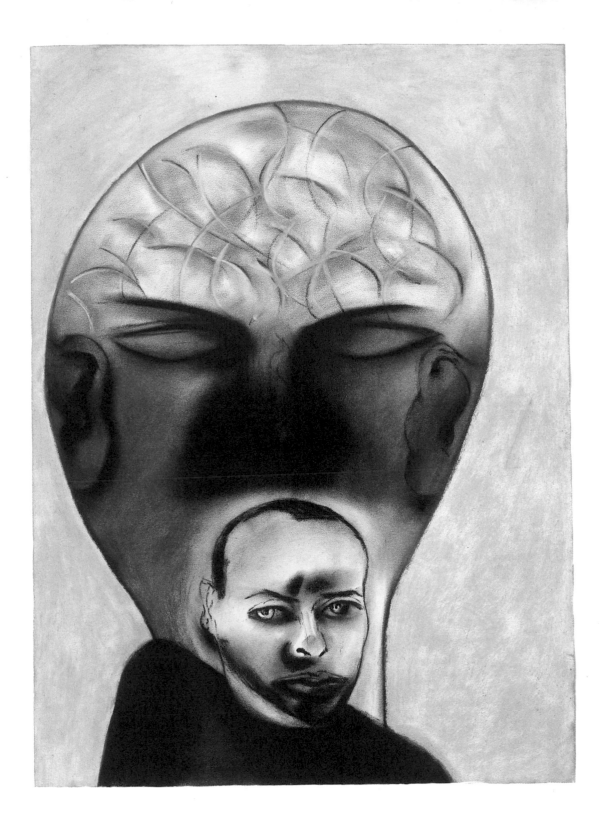

Abbraccio, 1983
Pastel on Rives paper
26 x 19″ (66 x 48.2 cm)
Private Collection, Courtesy Galerie Bruno
Bischofberger, Zurich

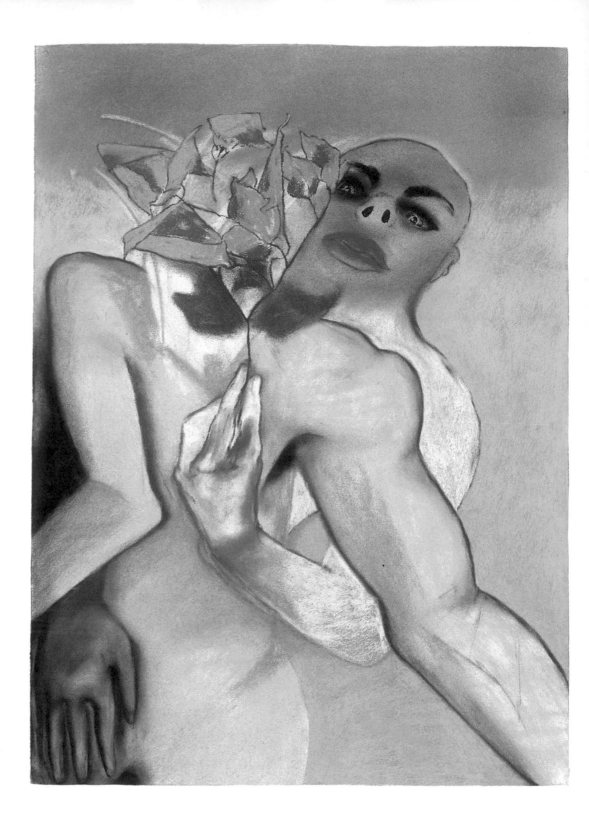

Everything I Know, 1983
Pastel on Rives paper
26 x 19″ (66 x 48.2 cm)
Private Collection, Courtesy Galerie Bruno
Bischofberger, Zurich

Three Dead Soldiers, 1983
Pastel on Rives paper
26 x 19″ (66 x 48.2 cm)
Private Collection, Courtesy Galerie Bruno
Bischofberger, Zurich

Naso, 1983
Pastel on Rives paper
26 x 19″ (66 x 48.2 cm)
Collection of Francesco and Alba Clemente,
New York

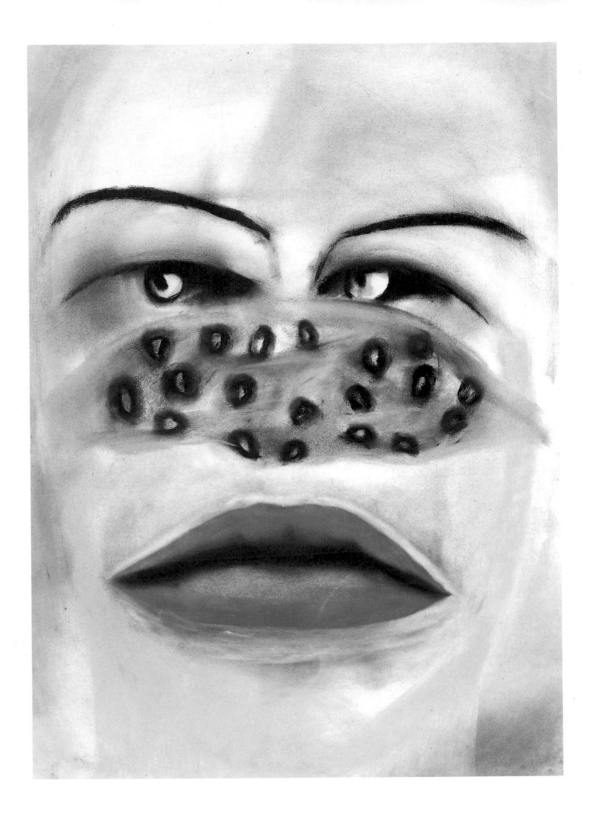

Italy, 1983
Pastel on Rives paper
26 x 19″ (66 x 48.2 cm)
Philadelphia Museum of Art. Purchased:
Hunt Manufacturing Co. Arts Collection
Program. 1984-8-1

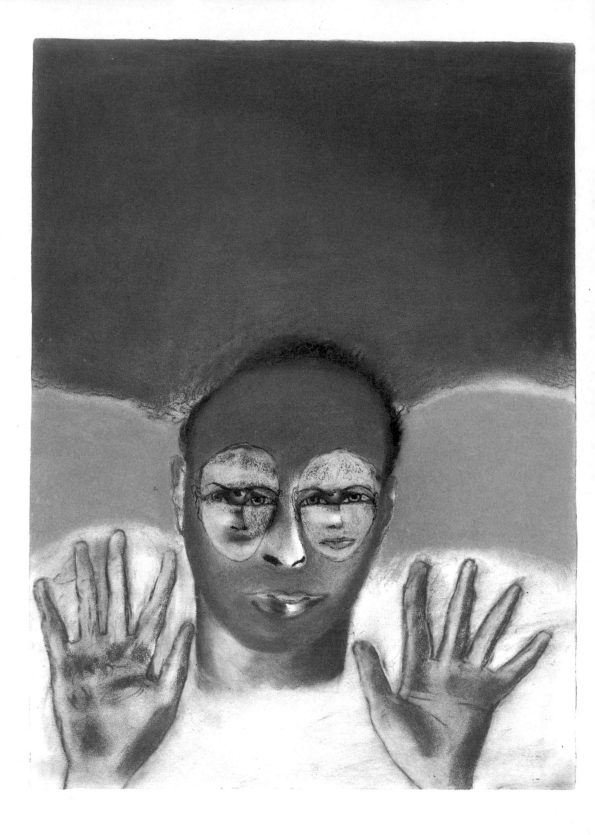

Kiss, 1983
Pastel on Rives paper
26 x 19″ (66 x 48.2 cm)
Collection of Francesco and Alba Clemente,
New York

The Celtic Bestiary, 1984
Series of eight pastels on Rives paper
each 26 x 19″ (66 x 48.2 cm)
Collection of Gerald S. Elliott, Chicago

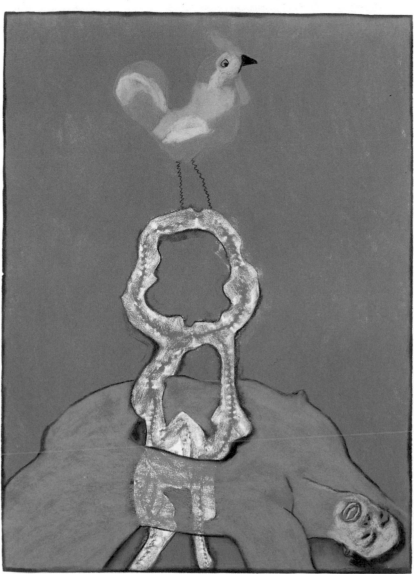

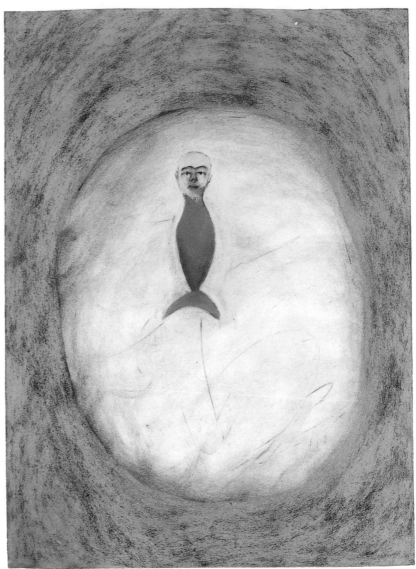

Six of a series of forty drawings created to
accompany "Hemispheres," a dance
performance by Molissa Fenley, 1983
India ink on Japanese paper
each approximately 6 x 8″ (15.2 x 20.3 cm)
Collection of Francesco and Alba Clemente,
New York

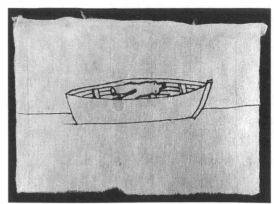
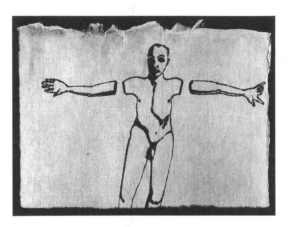

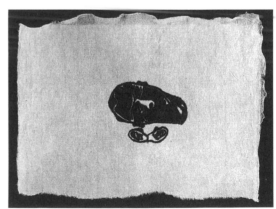

Chimayo, no. 16 from the series
Two Garlands, 1986
Oil monotype on Japanese paper
49 x 32″ (124.5 x 81.3 cm) (sheet),
36³/₁₆ x 20¹/₁₆″ (91.9 x 51 cm) (image)
Courtesy Thomas Ammann, Zurich

Poem, no. 28 from the series
Two Garlands, 1986
Oil monotype on Japanese paper
49 x 32″ (124.5 x 81.3 cm) (sheet),
36³/₁₆ x 20¹/₁₆″ (91.9 x 51 cm) (image)
The Museum of Modern Art, New York.
Associate Council Fund. 305.86

Memory, no. 36 from the series
Two Garlands, 1986; poem, "A Glimpse,"
by John Wieners
Oil monotype on Japanese paper
49 x 32″ (124.5 x 81.3 cm) (sheet),
36³/₁₆ x 20¹/₁₆″ (91.9 x 51 cm) (image)
Collection of Raymond Foye, New York

Mother, no. 76 from the series
Two Garlands, 1986
Oil monotype on Japanese paper
49 x 32″ (124.5 x 81.3 cm) (sheet),
36³/₁₆ x 20¹/₁₆″ (91.9 x 51 cm) (image)
Collection of Joshua Mack,
Byram, Connecticut

Generation, no. 87 from the series
Two Garlands, 1986
Oil monotype on Japanese paper
49 x 32″ (124.5 x 81.3 cm) (sheet),
36³/₁₆ x 20¹/₁₆″ (91.9 x 51 cm) (image)
Private Collection, Courtesy Sperone
Westwater, New York

Totality, no. 101 from the series
Two Garlands, 1986
Oil monotype on Japanese paper
49 x 32″ (124.5 x 81.3 cm) (sheet),
36³/₁₆ x 20¹/₁₆″ (91.9 x 51 cm) (image)
Collection of Francesco Pellizzi, New York

Misunderstanding, no. 105 from the series
Two Garlands, 1986
Oil monotype on Japanese paper
49 x 32″ (124.5 x 81.3 cm) (sheet),
36³/₁₆ x 20¹/₁₆″ (91.9 x 51 cm) (image)
Collection of Francesco Pellizzi, New York

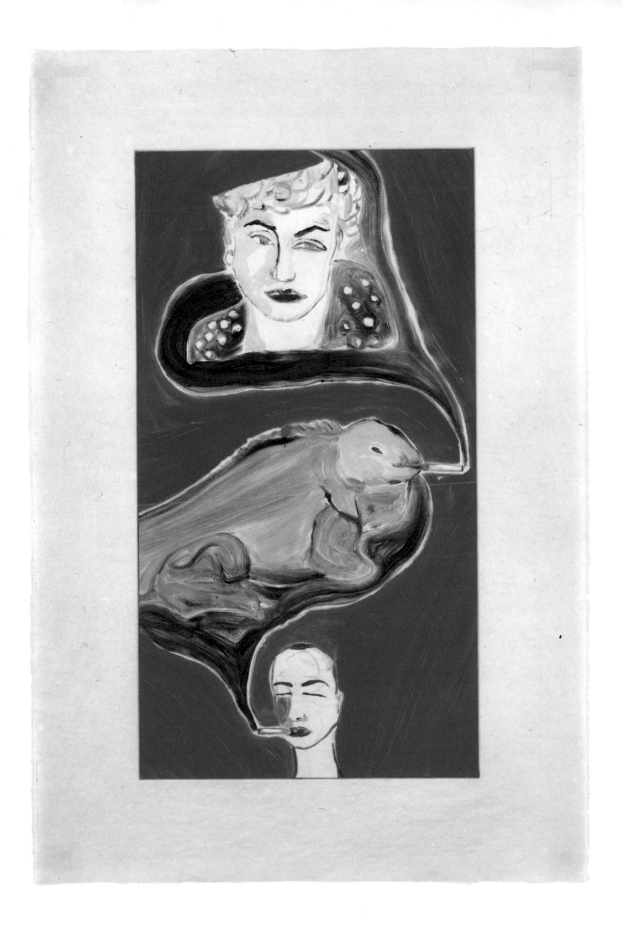

173   New York

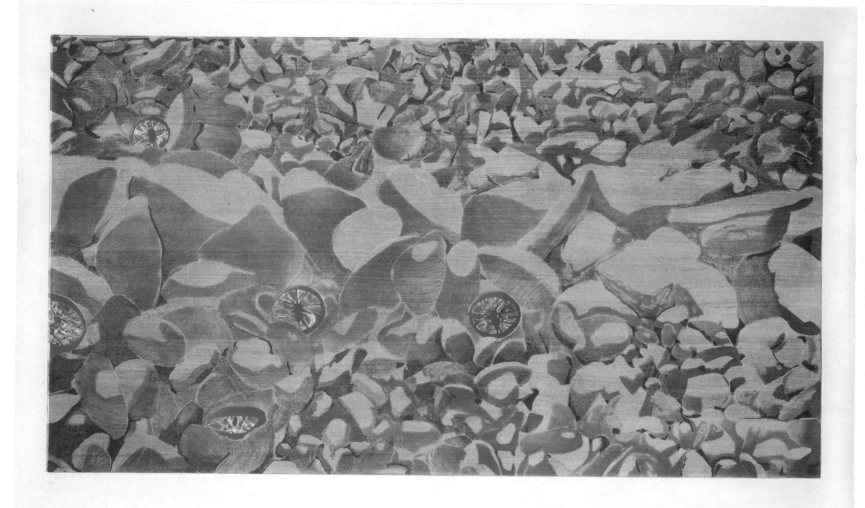

Sky, 1985
Spitbite, aquatint, and soft- and hard-ground
etching on Somerset paper
41 x 65″ (104.1 x 165.1 cm) (sheet),
34 x 59″ (86.4 x 149.9 cm) (plate)
Artist's proof 8; edition of 35 and 15 artist's
proofs; printed by Hidekatsu Takada and
Marcia Bartholme at Jeryl Parker Editions,
New York; published by Crown Point Press,
San Francisco
Crown Point Press, San Francisco and New
York

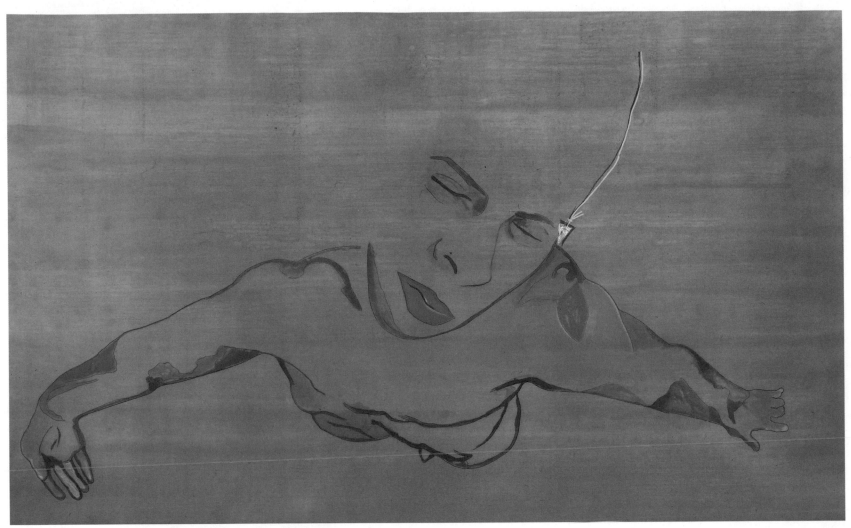

Semen, 1987
Etching, aquatint, and drypoint on Rosaspina
paper with silver attachment
54 x 90½" (137.2 x 229.9 cm) (sheet),
40⅝ x 66⅜" (103.2 x 168.6 cm) (plate)
Edition 31/55; printed by Vigna Antoniniana,
Rome; published by 2 RC Editions, Rome
Petersburg, London and New York

One to Five, 1987
Series of five soft-ground etchings on J. B.
Green Renaissance paper
each 25½ x 20″ (64.8 x 50.8 cm) (sheet),
15½ x 15½″ (39.4 x 39.4 cm) (plate)
Edition 12/50; printed by Maurice Payne, New
York; published by Raymond Foye Editions,
Ltd., New York
Philadelphia Museum of Art. Purchased with
funds contributed by Marion Stroud Swingle.
1990-12-1—5

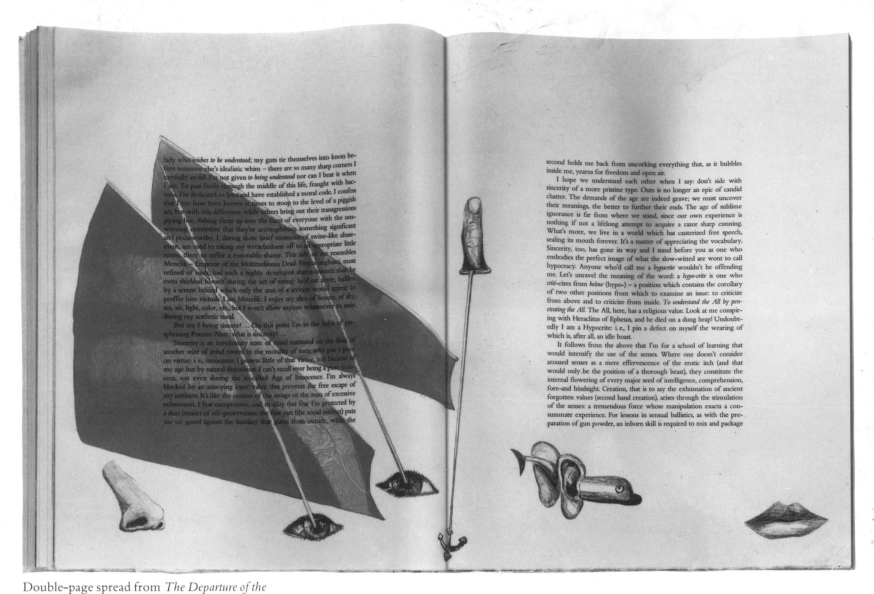

Double-page spread from *The Departure of the Argonaut*; Italian text by Alberto Savinio, 1917 (English translation by George Scrivani, 1986), and lithographs by Francesco Clemente, 1983, 1985, 1986
Book of bound letterpress and lithographs on mold-made Okawara kozo paper
25³/₄ x 20″ (65.4 x 50.8 cm) (sheet)
Edition 96/200; printed by the workshop of Rolf Neumann, Stuttgart; published in 1986 by Petersburg Press, New York
Philadelphia Museum of Art. Purchased: Gertrude Schemm Binder Fund and funds contributed by Marion Stroud Swingle.
1986-93-1

By the Sea, 1986
Lithograph on mold-made Okawara kozo
paper (in three parts)
25⅞ x 79⅛″ (65.7 x 201 cm)
Artist's proof 14; edition of 100 and 20 artist's
proofs; printed by Perry Tymeson, New York;
published by Petersburg Press, New York
Petersburg, London and New York

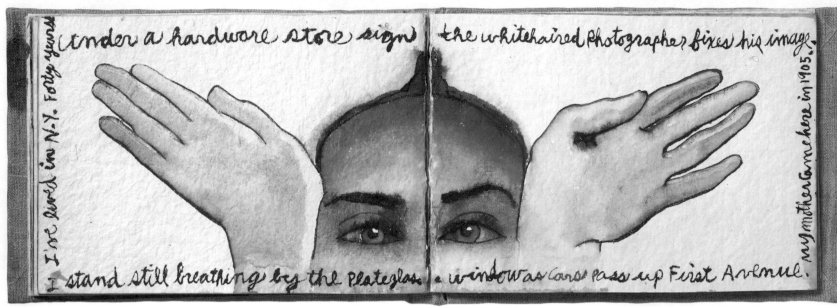

Double-page spread from *Images from Mind and Space*; text by Allen Ginsberg and illustrations by Francesco Clemente, 1983
Book of fifteen bound sheets in watercolor on paper
5⅝ x 7¹³/₁₆" (14.3 x 19.8 cm) (sheets), 6 x 8¼" (15.2 x 21 cm) (bound)
Collection of Francesco and Alba Clemente, New York

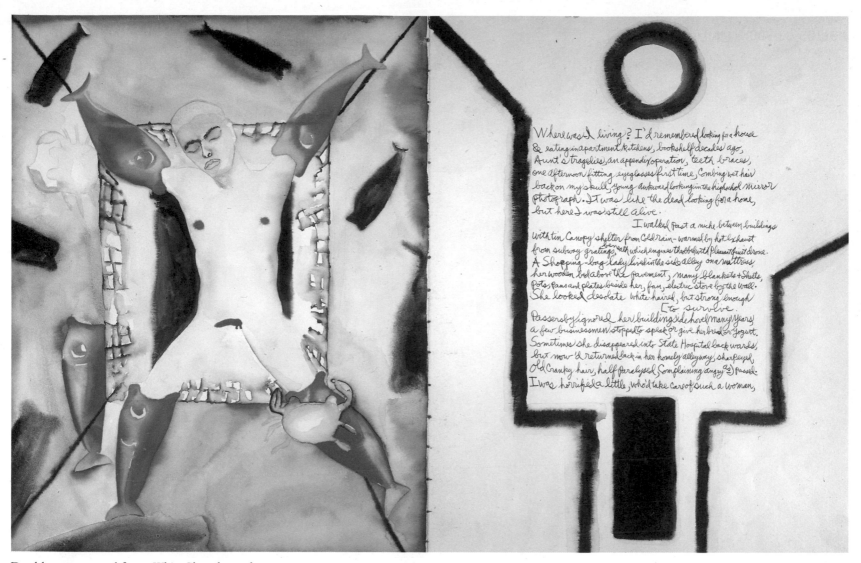

Double-page spread from *White Shroud*; text by
Allen Ginsberg and illustrations by Francesco
Clemente, 1983
Book of eight unbound sheets in ink, pencil,
and watercolor on Fabriano paper
17½ x 13½" (44.4 x 34.3 cm) (single sheet),
17½ x 26¾" (44.4 x 67.9 cm) (double sheet)
Collection of Jean Pigozzi, Lausanne

Page from *Early Morning Exercises*; text by
John Wieners and illustrations by Francesco
Clemente, 1984
Book of eleven unbound sheets in ink, pencil,
watercolor, colored pencil, and metallic paint
on paper, pasted onto color reproductions of
Indian paintings from the album *Kishangarh
Painting* (Lalit Kalā Series Portfolio No. 22,
1981)
17 x 13" (43.2 x 33 cm)
Collection of Francesco and Alba Clemente,
New York

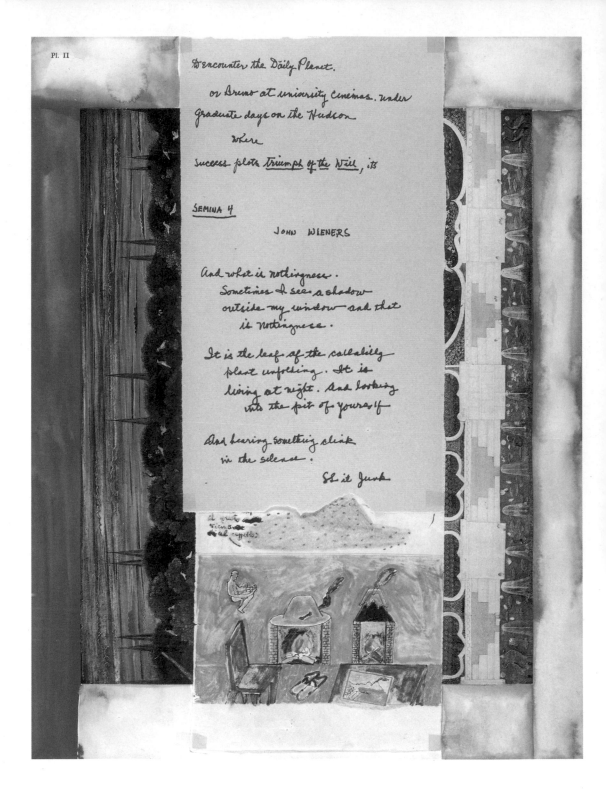

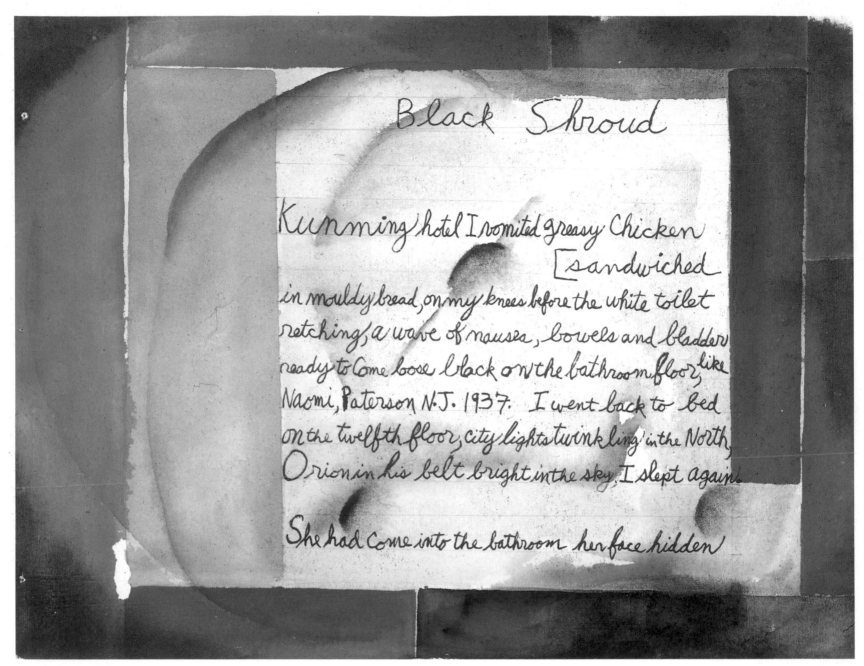

Page from *Black Shroud*; text by Allen Ginsberg, 1984, and illustrations by Francesco Clemente, 1985
Book of six unbound sheets in ink, pencil, and watercolor on paper
10½ x 13¾" (26.7 x 34.9 cm)
Collection of Francesco and Alba Clemente, New York

Trophy, 1990
Pastel on paper
26³/₁₆ x 40³/₁₆" (66.5 x 102 cm)
Private Collection, Courtesy Anthony d'Offay
Gallery, London

Bibliographic Note

Francesco Clemente's bibliography and exhibition history are extensive, and the principal references through the mid-1980s are published in the exhibition catalogues *Francesco Clemente: Pastelle 1973–1983*, edited by Rainer Crone, with essays by Rainer Crone, Zdenek Felix, Lucius Grisebach, and Joseph Leo Koerner (Munich, 1984); and *Francesco Clemente*, by Michael Auping, with an essay by Francesco Pellizzi in collaboration with Jean-Christophe Ammann (New York, 1985). An extensive bibliographic file on the artist is maintained by the Sperone Westwater gallery in New York. Especially useful are four published interviews with Clemente: Robin White, "Francesco Clemente," *View*, vol. 3, no. 6 (November 1981); Giancarlo Politi, "Francesco Clemente," *FlashArt*, no. 117 (April–May 1984), pp. 12–21; Rainer Crone and Georgia Marsh, *Clemente: An Interview with Francesco Clemente* (New York, 1987); and Lisa Phillips, "Exposition Clemente: Les Chemins de la sagesse," *Beaux Arts Magazine*, no. 69 (June 1989), pp. 91–95, 159–60, with an English summary. Also helpful are Edit deAk, "Francesco Clemente," *Interview*, vol. 12, no. 4 (April 1982), pp. 68–70; and Donald Kuspit, "Clemente Explores Clemente," *Contemporanea*, vol. 2, no. 7 (October 1989), pp. 36–43.

The following is a selection of the books, articles, and exhibition catalogues that have proven useful in approaching Clemente's work in general, particularly his works on paper: Edit deAk, "A Chameleon in a State of Grace," *Artforum*, vol. 19, no. 6 (February 1981), pp. 36–41; Galerie Bruno Bischofberger, *Francesco Clemente: Watercolours* (Zurich, 1982), with an introduction by Rainer Crone; The Museum of Modern Art, New York, *New Work on Paper 2: Jonathan Borofsky, Francesco Clemente, Mario Merz, A. R. Penck, Giuseppe Penone* (July 28–September 21, 1982), catalogue by Bernice Rose; Heiner Bastian, ed., *Sandro Chia, Francesco Clemente, Enzo Cucchi* (Bielefeld, 1983), with an introduction by Wolfgang Max Faust; Whitechapel Art Gallery, London, *Francesco Clemente: The Fourteen Stations* (January 7–February 20, 1983), with a foreword by Nicholas Serota and essays by Henry Geldzahler and Mark Francis (also shown at Groninger Museum, Groningen [April 1–May 8, 1983]; Badischer Kunstverein, Karlsruhe [May 24–July 3, 1983]; and Moderna Museet, Stockholm [September 17–October 30, 1983]); Kestner-Gesellschaft Hannover, *Francesco Clemente: Bilder und Skulpturen* (December 7, 1984–January 20, 1985), edited by Carl Haenlein; Paul Gardner, "Gargoyles, Goddesses and Faces in the Crowd," *ARTnews*, vol. 85, no. 3 (March 1985), pp. 52–59; The Metropolitan Museum of Art, The Mezzanine Gallery, New York, *An Exhibition and Sale: Francesco Clemente, Prints 1981–1985* (May 14–June 9, 1985), with an introduction by Henry Geldzahler and an interview with Clemente by Danny Berger; David Shapiro, Francesco Pellizzi, and Rainer Crone, "Collaboration: Francesco Clemente," *Parkett*, no. 9 (1986), pp. 16–81; Anthony d'Offay Gallery, *Francesco Clemente: Pastels 1980* (London, 1986); *Francesco Clemente: India* (Pasadena, 1986); Sperone Westwater, *Francesco Clemente: Two Garlands* (New York, 1986); Fundación Caja de Pensiones, Madrid, *Francesco Clemente affreschi: Pinturas al fresco* (April 7–May 17, 1987), with essays by Henry Geldzahler, Rainer Crone, and Diego Cortez; Dieter Koepplin, *Francesco Clemente CVIII: Watercolours Adayar 1985* (Zurich, 1987 [English text, Zurich, 1988]); and Robert Storr, "Realm of the Senses," *Art in America*, vol. 75, no. 11 (November 1987), pp. 132–45, 194. A list of publications in which many of Clemente's early works are illustrated is given in n. 15 on p. 25 above. Recent pastels are reproduced in Anthony d'Offay Gallery, *Francesco Clemente: Purification of the Twelve* (London, 1987); Francesco Clemente and Robert Creeley, *IT* (Zurich, 1989); and Francesco Clemente and Rene Ricard, *Sixteen Pastels* (London, 1989).

A.P.

Index of
Illustrations

Photographic Credits

Jeannette Montgomery Barron, New York, Figure 52;
Leo Castelli Gallery, New York, Figure 8; Geoffrey
Clements, New York, Figure 41; Giorgio Colombo,
Milan, p. 30 (top), Figures 11, 12; Kathleen Culbert-
Aguilar, Chicago, p. 150; Prudence Cuming Associates
Ltd., London, pp. 40, 65–68, 83–86, Figures 4, 7, 28;
Raymond Foye, New York, Figures 23, 46; Allen Gins-
berg, New York, p. 112, Figures 38, 50, 51, 53; Tom
Haartsen, Figure 6; Andrew Harkins, pp. 182, 183,
Figures 9, 10, 16, 21, 22, 24, 33; Bill Jacobson Studio, p.
149; Erik Landsberg, p. 179; courtesy The Pace Gallery,
New York, p. 149; Francesco Pellizzi, New York, Figures
20, 43; Phillips/Schwab, New York, Figure 44; courtesy
Sperone Westwater, New York, pp. 71, 73, 162–65; John
Stoel, Groningen, Figure 13; Jim Strong, Inc., p. 152;
courtesy Jack Tilton Gallery, New York, Figure 2; courtesy John Weber Gallery, New York, Figure 1; Wolfgang
Wesener, New York, Figure 37; Graydon Wood, pp. 29,
45–47, 62, 63, 70, 72, 78, 130 (left), 159, 160, 176–78, 180,
181; Dorothy Zeidman, New York, pp. 80–81, Figures
17–19, 29–32, 34, 36, 48, 49; Dorothy Zeidman, New
York, courtesy Sperone Westwater, New York, pp. 168–
73; Alan Zindman, New York, Figure 40; Zindman/
Fremont, New York, p. 161, Figures 42, 45.
Other photographs supplied by the owners.

Designed by Nathan Garland, New Haven, Connecticut

Composition by Southern New England Typographic Service, Hamden, Connecticut

Printed and bound in Italy by Stamperia Valdonega, Verona